SECRET
INLAND EMPIRE

A GUIDE TO THE WEIRD, WONDERFUL, AND OBSCURE

Larry Burns

Copyright © 2019, Reedy Press, LLC
All rights reserved.

Reedy Press
PO Box 5131
St. Louis, MO 63139
www.reedypress.com

No part of this publication may be reproduced or transmitted in any form or by
any means, electronic or mechanical, including photocopy, recording, or any
information storage and retrieval system, without permission in writing from the
publisher. Permissions may be sought directly from Reedy Press at the above
mailing address or via our website at www.reedypress.com.

Library of Congress Control Number: 2018962609
ISBN: 9781681062044

Design by Jill Halpin
Unless otherwise indicated, all photos are courtesy of the author
or in the public domain. Photo page 89 courtesy of Jessica Duenow.

Printed in the United States of America
19 20 21 22 23   5 4 3 2 1

DEDICATION

To all immigrants. This book would be blank pages without your stories, your sweat, and your sacrifice. Don't stop coming. We want you, and we need you.

CONTENTS

ACKNOWLEDGMENTS

Thank you to the places that provided space for me to write when I couldn't work from home: Back to the Grind Coffeehouse and the Glenn Hunt Center at Riverside City College. Your people and your coffee kept the words flowing.

Thanks to people who sat for interviews and freely shared their knowledge and expertise: Kevin Bash, Barbara Burns, Deborah Clifford, Lucas Cuny, Julie Frederickson, Jeffrey Harmon, Garner Holt, Steve Lech, Ruth McCormick, Douglas McCulloh, Sally McManus, Nancy Melendez, Pat Murkland, Albert Okura (aka The Chicken Man), Connie Ransom, Jim Rawitsch, Phil Rosentrater, Megan Suster, and Miguel Tarango. Thanks as well to Grandma Burns and Gran Goldware, who watched my daughter so I could get out and explore. And to Steve Veen, thank you for joining me on the road for some of the more "far out" destinations. You've been a cool dude and friend since fourth grade.

Most of all, thanks to my wife, Rebeccah Goldware, my future partner in crime and the smartest person I know.

INTRODUCTION

Where exactly is the Inland Empire? Rather than answer that question, this book attempts to share a picture of the IE based on its shared values, experience, and culture. Lines on a map offer little useful information. Borders are merely choices, and this book chooses to ignore those and instead cast a wide net to capture creative cultural expressions as diverse as people of the IE. If, however, you prefer geographic maps over philosophical ones, consider the Inland Empire to include Riverside and San Bernardino counties—and maybe a step or two beyond. Where is the Inland Empire? Where you least expect it.

What does the Inland Empire offer? For starters, mountains with hundreds of trails for hiking, skiing, and mountain biking. And deserts holding some of the IE's oldest artifacts and plenty of its wonderful artistic creations. Our national parks and preserves will ensure that what's offered now will be available for future generations, too. Working behind the scenes, IE scientists are literally saving endangered species, while engineers continue to tinker and invent contraptions that sometimes confound, but often improve living conditions around the world.

Who are these people? They're the Native Americans who settled these lands thousands of years ago, as well as the Indians who were forced here. They include the Californios and Americans, as well as immigrants from Central and South America, and Europe. The promise of health and wealth and security in the Golden State attracted the industrious, the creative, the far-out, and the weary. This place called to them, and they responded by moving here, dragging friends along, and creating new things together. People of all creeds arrived with big plans and shovels in hand to turn some soil. All of them left their mark in this wonderous place.

1 GOOD FENCES MAKE GOOD NEIGHBORS

Where do we put all these houses?

Standing at the corner of East Baseline Road and North Meridian Avenue places you at the nexus of Southern California. Every single plot of land in Southern California was measured from this point. No kidding! The entire basin "begins" at this forgotten corner of the Inland Empire. Put another way, it's "the place" of Inland Southern California that makes all the other places possible.

The contemporary Inland Empire originated as a stop between the early eastern United States and that glimmer to the west that is Los Angeles. The region was settled by waves of immigrants, along with dream makers, refuge seekers, and those who simply wished to create a better world than where they came from. Following the Civil War, veterans from both sides of the conflict sought out new territories as blank canvases to script new lives. Unlike the multiple nomadic and permanent Indian societies going back at least five thousand years, this new wave of immigrants believed strongly in personal ownership of land. This required some rules and standards as to how the "new lands" should be divided and developed.

ONE [BASELINE] TO RULE THEM ALL

WHAT Way more than a line in the sand

WHERE Corner of East Baseline Road and North Meridian Avenue, border of Rialto and San Bernardino, in San Bernardino

COST Free

PRO TIP A leisurely drive west to where Baseline merges with Route 66 takes about one hour.

The valley's heat waves made visibility difficult, so Col. Washington's men lit huge fires and did the surveys at night. Small changes to the street name "Baseline" "Base Line" "Baseline Rd" Baseline Ave" appear as the survey road moves across the cities of the Inland Empire. Photos courtesy of Larry Burns.

At its western end, it connects with another historical road, Route 66.

Accordingly, planning was undertaken to establish an east-west "baseline" measurement of lands acquired by the United States following the Mexican-American War. Next, the bisecting north-south line was delineated and named "meridian." The original marker laid by the survey team—constructed of banded iron and wood, and strung against three trees—was reduced to rubble many years ago. Rumors hint that pieces of that marker may be "hidden" in one of the area's museums. That marker was placed by Col. Henry Washington in November 1852. As a US deputy surveyor, he literally put the Inland Empire on the map!

2 THE ROAD THAT UNITED RIVERSIDE COUNTY

Where are you going? Where have you been?

In this era of Google Maps and self-driving cars, Jack Rabbit Trail is a reminder that it used to take planning, risk-taking, and considerable mechanical skills to cross the Inland Empire by automobile. In an area known as the Badlands lies a reminder of what it took to command the driver's seat.

The road is a fitting Inland Empire creation. Put together quickly to address a pressing need, it was constructed by locals with a passion that outstripped their expertise. But it got the job done: establishing a road linking all the cities that made up Riverside County to the county seat in Riverside.

Here's where the story gets into "three little pigs" territory. The first road was built in 1897 along the valley, on compressed soil, and filled with hairpin curves and roller-coaster slopes; picture a rural version of Lombard Street in San Francisco, strung across several miles. Version two was better positioned and engineered, but the lack of pavement made it impassable when it rained. In 1924, it was paved, creating the first 100-percent paved route a vehicle could navigate from Los Angeles to Palm Springs.

THE BADLANDS' JACK RABBIT TRAIL

WHAT A decaying representation of transportation innovation

WHERE Highway 60 West at the Jack Rabbit Trail exit, Riverside County

COST Free

PRO TIP Four-wheel drive or high-clearance vehicles are ideal for portions of this road trip. Caution: Do not drive this road after dark!

4

In 1986, Riverside County removed this road from it's maintained roads database, so each year the pass erodes just a bit more. As the first paved road between LA and Palm Springs, a car ride in 1924 was a breeze in just under 4 hours. Photos courtesy of Larry Burns.

By 1936, Highway 60 made the road a much less palatable option. Today, there are many ways to cross the desert, each one a bit faster than the last. But if your objective is to learn something along the way, take this scenic detour around the Badlands. The road is no longer maintained, but most is still drivable. Just take it slow, and take some extra water.

The first road, built ad hoc by a pair of county supervisors, lacked respect for private property and personal safety, but it scored big points for its moxie.

A LOCAL FOODS SOURCE —AND SO MUCH MORE

How well do you know your taco history?

Although many may never set foot in the Inland Empire, it is impossible to miss the region's culinary contributions. Several of the world's largest fast-food chains originated in the IE. Where did all that innovation start? This café! In addition to its record as the oldest continuously operating Mexican food restaurant in San Bernardino County, Milta Café is also the place that inspired the hard-shell, ground beef taco popularized by Taco Bell itself.

Milta Café has thrived through the high times and the trying times of the community. You can see parts of that history come alive the moment you step across the café's fabled doorway. They were part of the locally sourced food movement before there was a name for it. From their opening in 1937, family recipes and a generous, sharing spirit have earned them generations of fans. The most famous fan of them all was fellow restaurateur Glen Bell.

Bell, who went on to open Taco Bell restaurants across the country, was intrigued by the long lines that formed daily for lunch and dinner at the cafe. Milta's tantalizing tacos were all the rage. In a moment that must leave many a patent attorney reaching for the antacids, Bell befriended the family and staff, and "discovered" the secrets of these crispy concoctions.

MILTA CAFÉ

WHAT A restaurant serving quality comfort foods from the same spot since 1937

WHERE 602 N Mount Vernon Ave., San Bernardino

COST $6–$12 for a full meal

PRO TIP The menu includes traditional American fare. Hours: 9 a.m.–8 p.m. daily; closed Monday.

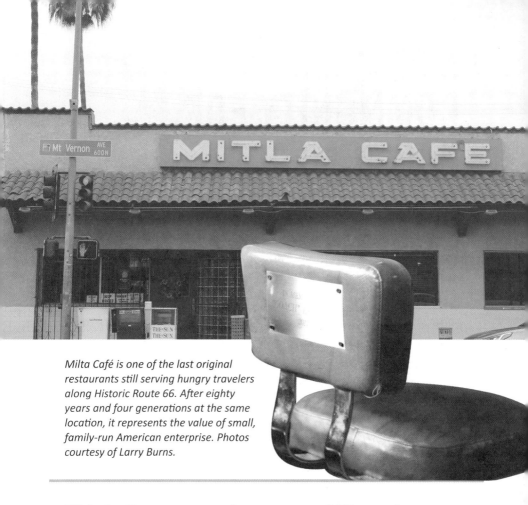

Milta Café is one of the last original restaurants still serving hungry travelers along Historic Route 66. After eighty years and four generations at the same location, it represents the value of small, family-run American enterprise. Photos courtesy of Larry Burns.

This is the unassuming nexus of Hispanic industry, entertainment, and political power.

Amazingly, founder Lucia Rodriguez held no grudge and refused to sue for her rightful compensation. Proof that she chose the correct path? Her dream restaurant is still strong, still serving food that people love, and still family owned and operated. Try to find a fast-food story with a happier ending.

Don't settle for the simulation. Grab a plate of the real deal; in doing so, you'll recognize something special about the Inland Empire. Its people are caring and generous—and operate according to values that will last longer than fame and riches.

4 A RETIREMENT COMMUNITY FOR HAPPY MEAL TOYS

What's the happiest part of your meal?

Were it not for the efforts of Albert Okura, aka "The Chicken Man," this place would be an empty lot. As the founder of the food chain Juan Pollo, Okura has an interest in fast-food history. Working with the City of San Bernardino, he rededicated this landmark as a public museum, fifty years to the day after the McDonald brothers served their first fifteen-cent hamburger in 1947.

Thousands of toys, displayed by era and genre, share the shelves with actual pieces from classic McDonald's shops. You can't ride the merry-go-round (alas!), but it may bring back fond memories if you're over forty. The artifacts are a mixture of loans and donations, many from franchise owners. The hope is to one day display an example of every toy ever sold in a Happy Meal.

Like the artifacts inside, the four-walled, wrap-around, exterior mural is a do-it-together project. Several pieces were completed by guest artists. Recent brushes with

THE WORLD'S FIRST MCDONALD'S RESTAURANT

WHAT Inland Empire history featured in food, art, and industry

WHERE 1398 N "E" St., San Bernardino

COST Free

PRO TIP Bring or send in a picture of you with McDonald's swag, and you could be featured in the museum, too. Hours: 10 a.m.–5 p.m. daily.

The mural includes dozens of historical secrets, including a poster commemorating "the Rolling Stones" first US Tour date, in San Bernardino, CA, June 5th, 1964. Photo courtesy of Larry Burns.

fame include The Simpsons artist Phil Ortiz and Kevin Eastman, co-creator of the "Teenage Mutant Ninja Turtles." Artist, publisher, and all-around surrogate parent to hundreds of artistic endeavors, Phil Yeh, started an ambitious exterior design project that may never be finished. After Yeh was hired to do a small mural of San Bernardino history, the project ballooned, taking on a life of its own. It's moved beyond San Bernardino and features histories and timelines of significant places and peoples of the Inland Empire.

In a sense, it is a colorful illustration of this book that you hold in your hands. As a symbol, this building is an avatar of this region's spirit. It's an industrious artistic workhorse, one that starts small but builds over time into a dream needed by the larger world.

The exterior features Phil Yeh's "World's Most Detailed Mural."

5 SNACK ATTACK HISTORY

Did Guasti give birth to the multi-cultural snack food movement?

Richard Montañez has a fairly typical Mexican immigrant story. He grew up working among Guasti's vineyards. His early years in school were marked by his talent for business innovation and dual heritage as a Mexican and an American. On the first day of school, he was surprised to find he was the only kid with a burrito in his lunch sack instead of a sandwich. By the end of the first week, Montañez was selling dozens of twenty-five-cent burritos to his classmates.

Montañez had no idea he was connecting to a rich history of food entrepreneurship across the IE. Bakers, Juan Pollo, Farmer Boys, Del Taco, Taco Bell, and, of course, McDonald's all started with daring entrepreneurs who perfected their craft in the IE.

His march into snack-food stardom started with a motto: "Be the very best in all that you do, and trust what you know to see you through." That drive—combined with an open door policy at Frito-Lay, a division of PepsiCo that employed Montañez as a janitor—laid the groundwork for the creation of the single most popular snack food in the company's history: Flamin' Hot Cheetos.

Montañez took advantage of his janitorial job at the Rancho Cucamonga plant to learn Frito-Lay's business from top to bottom. His instincts about evolving American food tastes told

That town is now little more than shuttered buildings along an abandoned strip near Ontario International Airport.

Now all but abandoned, the town of Guasti was the worlds largest vineyard in 1917, producing over 5 million gallons of wine! The Flamin' Hot Cheeto remains one of Frito Lay's biggest sellers, surpassing the original Cheeto year after year. Photos courtesy of Larry Burns.

HOME OF FLAMIN' HOT CHEETOS

WHAT A forgotten town and an internationally famous snack food

WHERE 250 N Turner Ave., Ontario (San Secondo d'Asti)

COST Free to look at from outside

PRO TIP San Secondo d'Asti Catholic Church, built by Secondo Guasti, was inspired by a church from his hometown, Asti, Italy, and is the last publicly functioning structure of Guasti.

him there was a big gap in the product line: too few hot and spicy options.

Then, in 1991, a faulty machine created a batch of cheeseless Cheetos. Montañez, still a janitor, used those discards to prototype a custom blend of cheese and spices, his flaming hot idea, and pitch it to PepsiCo's CEO.

The result? Yet another local success story with worldwide impact. Montañez is now the vice president of multicultural sales for PepsiCo International, and Flamin' Hot Cheetos continue to outsell everything, even the original Cheeto.

<u>6</u> SCINTILLATING NEAR-CENTENNIAL OF DATE HISTORY

You know about the birds and bees, but what about the sex lives of dates?

The location has been the place to go for all things date related since 1924. That was the year that Boyd and Bess Shields left Los Angeles to be part of the newest agricultural craze in Indio: date farming. Never mind that they had zero experience in this industry. They had passion, strong young backs, and, of course, each other. Today, Shields continues innovating with new varieties, such as their hybridized Blonde and Brunette dates.

Date farming is daunting, to say the least; the task seems nearly impossible once a person understands the labor and capital required to grow that first date. From planting to first harvest is about a decade-long process. And that isn't even the most challenging part of the effort. Some would consider the date to be the English Bulldog of American agriculture because it can't reproduce on its own. So, this is not a gentleman's crop to be planted and ignored until harvest.

Extensive human intervention and protection are essential at every stage of date cultivation. For starters, the pollen from the male plant must be manually applied to each female flower. This kind of labor can't be left to mere bees.

SHIELDS DATE GARDEN

WHAT A desert fruit Eden decades in the making

WHERE 80225 US Hwy. 111, Indio

COST Free

PRO TIP After visiting the garden, enjoy refreshments at the café and check out the shop.

This recreated oasis demonstrates how early societies survived by finding water to support early agricultural efforts. Photo courtesy of Jessica Duenow.

An agile, fearless person must scale the tall tree, collect the pollen, then carefully apply it to a female tree. Care must be taken to remove thorns that can grow several feet each season. When the large bushels begin to appear, they must be covered to protect them from rain, which damages the fruit's delicate skin.

Over 90 percent of the world's dates come from this part of the Inland Empire.

7 THE SECRET SAUCE OF THE FAST-FOOD INDUSTRY

Is there a copyright on the phrase, "You want fries with that?"

Travel a bit, and you'll find that each corner of the globe lays claim to a notable achievement in food history. Italy tossed out the first pizza pie. China served ice cream a millennium before Baskin-Robbins. And the Inland Empire brought fast food to the world. Please drive forward to learn more.

The Golden Arches may be one of the most recognized symbols in the world. Residents of San Bernardino, were the first to taste the iconic burgers that the McDonald brothers began serving up in 1948. That location is still open, but it operates as a McDonald's Museum and features the "most detailed mural in the world," an ever-expanding canvas of rich Inland Empire history. Take a close look for some of these fast-food titans.

By far, Glen Bell left the widest mark in the industry. He started dozens of restaurants around Southern California, refusing to stick to one genre. Burgers, dogs, tacos—no food was safe from his entrepreneurial eye. With connections to nearly every fast-food innovation following World War II, Bell is the Kevin Bacon of value meals.

Bell's high-school classmate Neal Baker helped him open the first Bell's Burgers in 1948, the same year and the same city as McDonald's. By 1952, having cooked up his own burger dream, Baker opened Baker's Burgers in San Bernardino. His

FAST FOOD'S SILICON VALLEY

WHAT Birthplace of fast-food fortunes

WHERE Locations across the IE

COST Free

PRO TIP The first Naugles was in Riverside.

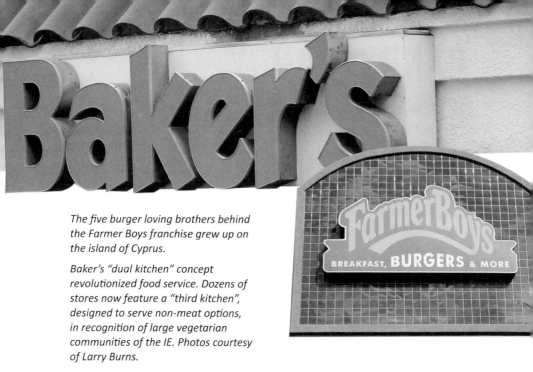

The five burger loving brothers behind the Farmer Boys franchise grew up on the island of Cyprus.

Baker's "dual kitchen" concept revolutionized food service. Dozens of stores now feature a "third kitchen", designed to serve non-meat options, in recognition of large vegetarian communities of the IE. Photos courtesy of Larry Burns.

innovation was the "twin kitchen," the first express kitchen split-designed to deliver Mexican and American fare.

Another Bell's Burgers graduate, Ed Hackbarth, quickly learned the ropes and moved north to open the first Del Taco in Yermo with David Jameson. A third partner, Dick Naugle, saw a winner and invested. But he left four years later to start Naugles, with similar items but a distinct flavor. That chain merged "back" into Del Taco in 1988.

Glen Bell opened a successful hot dog stand in 1961. Do you need to be told it was in San Bernardino? He wanted to focus on tacos and convinced John Galardi to buy his concept to mass-produce dogs and franchise stores around the country. Galardi branded the chain Weinerschnitzel.

Regional chains Bakers, Juan Pollo, Farmer Boys, and Burger Boss are recent additions to the IE's fast-food history.

8 CANDY, CANDY EVERYWHERE

You didn't think elves made all that, did you?

If you did something for eighty years, you'd probably get pretty good at it. Logan's Candies has been at it so long that some locals believe the Christmas holiday begins with that first seasonal lick of a Logan's peppermint stick. Generations have worn a path to this landmark, which in addition to peppermint and candy ribbons creates thousands of handmade chocolates for Valentine's Day or whenever you want to feel special.

Just off the main road of Euclid Avenue, the unassuming storefront hides a flurry of indoor activity. Allow yourself to be transported to a place that smells like the candy landscapes explored by Charlie Bucket and his friends in *Willy Wonka and the Chocolate Factory*.

Each year, Logan's Christmas tours and candy-making demonstrations are sold-out affairs; booking in July is highly recommended. But, oh, the secrets you'll hear about the creative process behind the most popular items! And as you learn about the intricate dance of fingers,

LOGAN'S CANDIES

WHAT The place Santa shops for handmade holiday treats

WHERE 125 W "B" St., Ontario

COST Free tours

PRO TIP Book a tour early; they usually fill up months in advance. Hours: Monday–Friday, 10 a.m.–6 p.m.; Saturday, 10 a.m.–5:30 p.m.

Since 1933, Logan's has satisfied the IE's love of the sweet stuff.

This handmade treat may be tough to beat, any larger and it would be impossible to construct and handle by hand. Since it's opening in 1933, Logan's has remained a small family run enterprise. Photos courtesy of Larry Burns.

wrists, and yes, hips required to make the perfect candy cane, you'll have plenty of freshly made confections to sample.

When you visit, take a selfie underneath the World's Largest Handmade Candy Cane, clocking in at over sixteen feet and thirty-six pounds; any larger would require a spotter and heavy equipment. No joke! And in addition to all the handmade holiday treats, you'll find traditional sweets, novelties, and ice cream by the scoop. No matter your craving, this family affair has been taking care of its customers since 1933.

CITRUS HISTORY IS CULTURAL HISTORY

Where might you discover a more complete history of citrus in the IE?

The fact that the Inland Empire (aka Orange Empire) was shaped by the orange is readily apparent. Plenty of the secrets in this book were made possible due to the innovations and practices required to create a profitable citrus industry. In much the same way that America's race to land on the moon spun off dozens of new enterprises, investments, and inventions, the Inland Empire's singular pursuit to bring fresh citrus to the world literally built many of the communities existing to this day.

Chronicles of those achievements often deemphasized or outright ignored the African American contribution to that success. That's why the work of the Relevancy and History Project could not have been launched at a better time. This pilot program (again, the Inland Empire is often a place to innovate and try new things) conducts research through the collection of oral histories and related artifacts. UC Riverside, where David and Oscar Stokes provided guidance and labor in the establishment of the first orange groves, continues to work with the California State Parks system to answer a relevant question: What makes community?

For Riverside citrus, how it started was in large measure the labor and talent of Eliza Tibbets and John B. Adams. Tibbets acquired three Bahia Navel orange trees, and Adams was a highly

Masonic Orange Valley Lodge #13 was established in 1905 at Mercantile Hall (between Park and Howard at Twelfth Street). It served as a social hall and boardroom for Riverside's African American community.

The Relevancy and History Project was recently featured on Humanities for All, a website that showcases the full range of publicly engaged humanities work at higher education institutions across the United States. Explore their site to learn more about how nationwide publicly engaged humanities research, teaching, preservation, and programming have advanced humanities scholarship and enriched American life. Photo courtesy of Larry Burns.

respected "budder," someone who can do the delicate task of grafting budwood onto rootstock. For the nonagriculturally savvy, this is how new trees are created. And that's exactly how Riverside's citrus industry went from three gift trees to the countless acres of prosperity it is today.

A bit later, in 1874, Israel "Doc" Beal of Redlands purchased twenty acres with money earned through years of hard labor. Those groves, as well as others around Redlands, provided the wealth to establish colleges, recreational space, and the housing necessary to sustain what grew into the Orange Empire.

THE RELEVANCY AND HISTORY PROJECT AT CALIFORNIA CITRUS STATE HISTORIC PARK

WHAT Recognition of the contributions of minority communities to agriculture and horticulture

WHERE 9400 Dufferin Ave., Riverside

COST $5 for parking; free tastes, tours, and education

PRO TIP Park rangers and docents can share dozens of other behind-the-scenes stories. When you visit, chat them up!

<u>10</u> WANT TO LIVE HERE? HERE'S YOUR PASS

"Well, how did I get here?"

Cajon Pass was a critical overland route for every successive wave of settlements to Inland Southern California. Precivilization, hunter-gatherer societies used the pass for thousands of years. In recent history, a six-hundred-year stretch roughly from the 1200s to the 1800s, the Serrano Indians settled this place, travelling into the surrounding lands as the seasons and food supplies dictated. The Mojave, significant traders regionally and across the Southwest, established paths as well. Captains of commerce, who established The Old Spanish Trail, followed the wisdom of previous generations by using this series of canyons.

Western expansion would not have been possible without this secret crossroads. Mormon communities became aware

---

THE MORMON ROCKS (AKA SERRANO ROCKS) AT CAJON PASS

WHAT Early IE transportation corridor

WHERE Mormon Rocks Fire Station/Trailhead, 7198 Abiel Barron Memorial Hwy., Phelan

COST Free

PRO TIP During severe snow events or "fire season," this road once again serves as a critical bypass around Interstate 15.

Spanish settlers claimed the Mojave Indians could travel up to one hundred miles a day at a trot, using this ancient "Main Street" of the IE.

The little holes found dotting these rocks are home to the smaller critters of the IE: birds, lizards, and many species of small mammals. Photo courtesy of Larry Burns.

of the beauty and resources thanks to a small military party that arrived near the end of the Mexican-American War. These communities traveled this well-worn path to establish the city of San Bernardino. But after a decade or so, they were "called home" to Salt Lake City.

Today, Cajon Pass is still a critical junction for the Inland Empire. High overhead, along Interstate 15, over forty-six million cars and eighteen-wheelers rumble past each year. Ironically, the traffic flow provided by cars and freight trucks has literally hidden the history of this place. Few realize there is anything below or that they are following a path established by the earliest Native American settlement of this region.

HIKE INTO HISTORY

How high can you get?

The Cahuilla Indians call this the home of Tahquitz—an easily angered trickster god trapped inside Tahquitz Rock. Inspiration for this tale could come from the regular lightning strikes that occur during storms. Those natural wonders are one of the reasons why the Fire Lookout, completed in 1937, is staffed only from Memorial Day until Thanksgiving—or until the first snowstorm of the season, whichever comes first!

Taking the shorter but strenuous 7.9-mile trip up and down from Idyllwild at the South Ridge Trailhead gives you more time to enjoy the panoramic views. If you have four-wheel drive, you can avoid walking the first half-mile from the main road to the trailhead, cutting a mile off your round-trip. From here, you can see south to the Palomar Mountains and Salton Sea of Imperial County. To the west, you can see well into Los Angeles County on clear days. But every day, you can recline atop the highest observation post of the San Bernardino National Forest at 8,846 feet above sea level.

About a third of the way up, stop at the large, smooth outcropping, covered in depressions that are each the size of a dinner plate. These mortar holes were used by Cahuilla Indians, and others, to mill grain to make flour. Hikers report finding metates as well; these are smooth, round stones that are often used to grind down materials in this slow process.

THE FIRE LOOKOUT AT TAHQUITZ PEAK

WHAT The highest observation post in the San Bernardino National Forest

WHERE Trail at South Ridge Trailhead at County Rd. 5S11, Idyllwild

COST $5 for a day pass

PRO TIP Ask for your "Squirrel Card" when you arrive as there's no giftshop at this peak. Your pledge to protect our natural resources will be your keepsake.

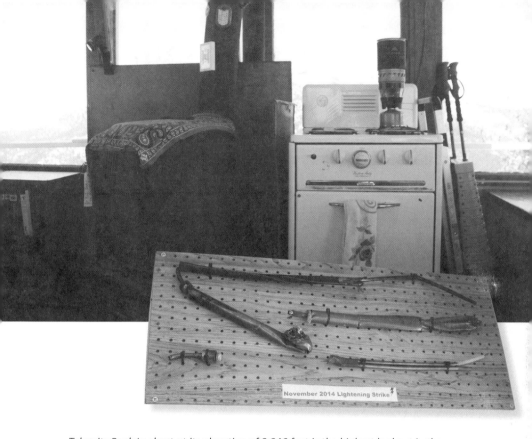

Tahquitz Peak Lookout at its elevation of 8,846 feet is the highest lookout in the San Bernardino National Forest. It is also the forest's longest continuously operated station, serving some 77 years, and is the only lookout located inside a Wilderness area. All work to maintain and repair this facility is done with manual labor only. No power tools are permitted in the wilderness area, including cordless. Photos courtesy of Larry Burns.

Fire lookouts, trained volunteers of the US Forest Service, call the little ten-foot-by-ten-foot tower home for several days at a time. When you visit, be sure to ask for a "tour" of the facility. You can see everything in a few minutes, but take time asking lots of questions to uncover all the secrets hidden when Tahquitz was encased in his stone prison by Cahuillian hero, Chief Algoot.

On a clear day, use this peak to see beyond the edges of the Inland Empire—no small feat!

AN IMPORTANT AND MYSTERIOUS RUNE

Is this a secret alien communication device?

These stones are not like the petroglyphs and pictographs found in the Mojave and Sonoran deserts. Those can be connected back to previous and current cultural groups and can be understood by studying historical records. These stones, by contrast, are found in no oral tradition of any existing cultural group. Their meaning, use, and origin may be the longest-running riddle of the Inland Empire.

Early speculation centered around their "Asian-like" appearance—understandable, because some of the symbols bear a passing resemblance to Sanskrit. Hence, an outlandish legend posited that the artifacts had been carved by shipwrecked Chinese sailors. Others gaze skyward for the answer, claiming it is a communication device left by space aliens. Given this area has many close encounters tales, there's more "evidence" to back this hypothesis.

In fact, using other artifacts found in the area, researchers have pegged the stone's age at between five hundred years old and upwards of three thousand years old. During this stretch of time, the only known inhabitants of the area were

---

THE HEMET MAZE STONE

WHAT An answer key in search of the right question

WHERE From State Hwy. 74, go north 3.2 miles on California Avenue to Maze Stone Park, Hemet

COST Free

PRO TIP Be mindful that parking is within a residential neighborhood. Avoid hiking during the hottest part of the day as there is limited shade for the one-third-mile trek up and back.

The "maze" consists of two rectangular boxes—one large and containing the other; centered. If one traces the patterns with different colored markers, one would find that between the boxes are two contiguous geometric patterns that resemble a maze. One "maze" is contained by the other on the left hand side. Photo courtesy of Larry Burns.

Native American Indian tribes. The Hemet Maze Stone is one of a few hundred that have been formally identified. This one is larger than the others uncovered. So far, stones bearing these markings appear only in a relatively small area that includes the Inland Empire, Imperial County, and San Diego County to the south.

This stone is the best preserved example and easiest to view of these stone tablets. A few more are uncovered each year and often left unmarked in the area.

13 SITE OF SOUTHERN CALIFORNIA'S ONLY COAL MINE

Is there gold in that thar hill?

Most people have heard of the California Gold Rush of 1848. Less well known is the discovery of coal in California about a half century later. The Inland Empire goes by many names, but "Coal Country" is not one of them. Nonetheless, the IE holds the record for the largest coal deposit ever found in the state.

It was unearthed by Madison Chaney, who spent many profitable years bringing up this rare find.

When the production began to fall, Chaney sold the rights to his mine for the then-handsome sum of ten thousand dollars. His payment arrived in the form of gold coins, fitting compensation for residents of the "Golden State." Soon afterwards, his wife became ill and died. In his grief he cursed God and the community, refusing to conduct a traditional funeral. By most accounts, he never got over her passing. Chaney grew increasingly reclusive, and he died a few years later in 1902. That's where the tale gets interesting.

Chaney left no will and zero clues as to the location of the gold. Rumor was that he'd never spent the gold. And because Chaney had no living relatives, the gold had to be somewhere

CHANEY HILL

WHAT A tale of found coal and lost gold

WHERE Jefferson Avenue at Grizzly Ridge Dr., Riverside County

COST Free

PRO TIP Forget looking for gold. There's more money to be made selling supplies to all the gold seekers.

Prospecting attracted thousands of people, but few gained Chaney's level of success and notoriety. Chaney Hill is just one of many secret or lost places to be discovered along historic Hwy 395. Photos courtesy of Larry Burns.

nearby, right? But despite extensive exploration over the century that followed, nobody ever laid claim to Chaney's gold.

As a gateway, this is a choice spot to discover where Murrieta, Wildomar, Rancho Temecula, and Rancho Laguna Grande all come together. If you visit, leave your shovel at home.

This gateway to Murrieta Valley is about the only section of road left unchanged by history.

27

14 NATURAL FORMATION LOOKS LIKE A GIANT ARROWHEAD

What's that sign say?

Every new arrival to the area has marveled at this naturally occurring feature set into the San Bernardino Mountains. The Arrowhead can be viewed across the valley, due to its relatively uniform white appearance, created by an abundance of white sage and quartz at this spot. It plays a key role in one of the origin stories of the Agua Caliente Indians. Those stories assign credit for the Arrowhead's creation to the God of Peace, who is said to have shot an arrow from the sky to mark a new place for the tribe to live in peace and prosperity.

THE ARROWHEAD

WHAT Part of the Agua Caliente Indians' origin story

WHERE Intersection of Waterman Avenue and Fortieth Street, off Highway 18, north of the softball field in Wildwood Park, San Bernardino

COST Free

PRO TIP Mormon settlers saw something different, calling this natural formation "The Spade."

Although the Arrowhead may not have delivered that particular promise into the modern age, it did represent a fresh start for many settlers. Nearby Arrowhead Hotel had several lively and interesting turns in its history. Like many places of recreation, it tried to capture that Hollywood flavor with film stars and as a place for people to behave badly away from Los Angeles. But like an aging film star, it waits, closed off and out of reach, for a graceful return to glory.

The Arrowhead can be viewed from many spots around the Inland Empire. There is an Arrowhead Peak hike, which

THE ARROWHEAD
MEASURES
1375 FEET LONG
449 FEET WIDE
AND IS AN AREA
OF 7.5 ACRES

Located in the foothills of the San Bernardino Mountains directly above the City of San Bernardino, the arrowhead landmark can be seen for miles around. This important landmark has for centuries been a symbol of the San Bernardino Valley to the Native Indians and then to the pioneers and settlers that followed. Indians who inhabited the San Bernardino Valley believed that the arrowhead pointed the way to the hot mineral springs below, with healing qualities, and thus considered it holy ground. Photos courtesy of Larry Burns.

can bring you up and over the Arrowhead. Simply park off Highway 18 near Crestline and look for the "Arrowhead Peak" trail head marker. The trail, while free, is rarely traveled and poorly maintained. If you go this way, bring a machete, water, and perhaps a sleeping bag. A much easier place for viewing the Arrowhead is from its national marker at Wildwood Park, just off Highway 18 in San Bernardino.

The Arrowhead points at the San Andreas Fault, a constant reminder that a major earthquake can occur at any time.

15 HEART OF STONE

Who crafted this mysterious message of love?

There's a lot to love about the outdoor recreation of the Inland Empire. The diversity of the region can be summed up in the common, unofficial message mentioned by many who promote the area: From the heart of the Inland Empire, you're a mere forty-five minutes from the mountains, the desert, and the beach.

Heart Rock Trail will put a smile on your face when you reach the destination—and not because you worked hard to get there. The hike in each direction is just under three-quarters of a mile. Another plus is the accessibility. Children and dogs do well on this path, which is fairly flat. Providing further comfort for those who don't get into the forests of the Inland Empire on a regular basis, the trail is marked with a variety of colorful, well-placed hearts and arrows painted at various spots. If you seek a friendly handshake and hearty welcome into the great outdoors, consider this place your friendly neighborhood greeter. A few hours in its shadow will leave you refreshed and feeling good about your decision to grab some fresh air and sunshine.

HEART ROCK TRAIL

WHAT An adorable natural formation in the forest near Crestline

WHERE Route 138, San Bernardino National Forest, Crestline (take the Camp Seeley turnoff)

COST Free

PRO TIP Nearby Camp Seeley was the setting for Disney's popular 1998 movie, *The Parent Trap.*

The waters, which often offer cool relief in the spring, are usually dry in the summer and fall.

A waterfall sometimes flows next to the heart, and when Seeley Creek is full, the waterfall also flows through the heart. Staying on the left hand ridge above the falls provides the best "bird's eye" view of this natural feature. Photos courtesy of Larry Burns.

As for the heart itself, the appearance is a result of natural water erosion. The water flow varies by season, but when water is running, there's a good-sized pool to wade in. At times, the water reaches and runs through the heart rock, but that becomes a rare sight during the seasonal dry periods. Other water features worth exploring include Seeley Creek and a natural slide that runs close to thirty feet.

16 I KNOW WE LEFT THE LAKE AROUND HERE SOMEWHERE!?

When is a lake not a lake?

In the dry climate of the Inland Empire, those who survived, and later thrived, knew where the water was. Famous Spanish explorer Juan Bautista de Anza described the lake as "several leagues in circumference and as full of white geese as water." But that was 1774. Changing climate and drastically increased water use has reduced the lake to part-time status.

With ephemeral lakes like Mystic Lake, the secret is knowing when to visit. Summer to fall, the lake retreats several feet a day. Rainfall and snowmelt runoff peaks around April, the best time to see this drying lake at its wettest.

Ample wildlife and access to fresh water are among the reasons why San Jacinto (established in 1870) is one of Riverside County's oldest cities. Raw materials from the nearby mountains and the area's agriculture contributed to its growth and sustainability.

The nearby areas support diverse outdoor recreation. Hunting is popular in this area, just as it was during the earlier periods of Indian settlement and Spanish exploration. Today, reservations and licenses are required and are available through the California Department of Fish and Wildlife. Waterfowl and pheasant are the most popular game in season, but one critter can be hunted year-round: the jackrabbit.

Today, these wetlands are part of the Pacific Flyover, a critical migratory-bird path stretching from South America to Alaska. The lake itself is part of the larger San Jacinto Wildlife Area, ensuring that these resources, although fleeting, will be here for years to come.

SAN JACINTO'S EPHEMERAL MYSTIC LAKE

The first recorded sighting of Mystic Lake is found in the journals of Juan Bautista de Anza, a Spanish explorer, who traveled through the area in 1774. Mystic Lake is located within the Pacific flyway and attracts upwards of 150 species of birds. Photos courtesy of Larry Burns.

WHAT A drying lake best seen in April

WHERE 17050 Davis St., Lakeview

COST $5 for a daily land pass; a permit and an additional fee are required for hunting

PRO TIP During rainy seasons, some of the dirt roads are difficult to navigate.

This is just one section of over nine thousand acres of the San Jacinto Wildlife Area.

17 DREAM STATE SHORE OF THE INLAND EMPIRE

How do you stay cool when the beach is miles away?

The history of the area is replete with stories of progress and growth, and no small number of imitators and hucksters who used the promise of the area for quick financial gain. Mentone Beach is an example of the grifter approach to development in the Inland Empire. These late-1800s charlatans left behind few lasting artifacts but plenty of entertaining tales.

Nearby communities like Redlands and Riverside would sell the health benefits of living here by shipping crates of oranges as well as postcards of idyllic natural settings and great expanses of prosperous looking agriculture—and plentiful water.

The creators of Mentone Beach had a desire to make money but lacked the real skills and assets to bring that about. So, they mirrored nearby success, printing up fake postcards and building this "beach" to impress investors who made the train ride west. The big-horn sheep and rocky-brown hillsides were transformed into lush green fields with herds of fluffy sheep and shade trees. The trick lasted only a few years, long enough for the creators to beat feet. But they left behind this cautionary tale, and a riptide and shark-free experience.

MENTONE BEACH

WHAT A getaway with an interesting history—but no sand

WHERE Mill Creek Rd., Mentone

COST Free (but BYO everything)

PRO TIP Be sure to wear sensible shoes as this "beach" has some rocky spots as well as a few thorns.

In San Bernardino County, opportunity-seeking land speculators found the perfect magnet for attracting frustrated Easterners fed up with the cold winters and humid summers back home. The dozens of small family farms and produce stands along Hwy 38 speak to this region's agricultural roots. Photos courtesy of Larry Burns.

When you've had enough fun in the sun, travel this main highway to catch other interesting sites. There are some folk art locations along Garnet Avenue near Mill Creek Road just minutes away. Along the main road, you'll find several roadside fruit and vegetable stands, which is what Mentone is best known for today.

Insider humor has spawned beach-themed restaurants, a liquor store, and folk art.

18 CROSS-COUNTRY SKIING

Where can you go to grab some winter cardio?

This place, nestled in the vast array of recreation around Big Bear and Bear Valley, is actually better known beyond the borders of the Inland Empire. Perhaps it remains a secret because it hosts spectacular mountain biking events most of the year. Given the changing climates, there are seasons when there's no snow—no machines creating the powder here, city slicker. So check conditions before you go.

The trail is a great place to introduce yourself to the Jeffrey pines found in all the area mountain ranges. One way to tell if you're near a Jeffrey pine is to take a sniff test. Get close to the bark, cup your hands with your nose as close as comfortable to the tree trunk, and inhale. Most people report a strong vanilla scent, like the last bites of a good diner pancake.

This is the great outdoors, so there are no food services along the trail. There are picnic areas and many other unofficial places to step off the trail a few feet and take a break, enjoy the views, and share a snack with some friends. Cross-country skiing is strenuous work, so it will be a much richer experience to tag along with family and friends. After the eighth time you fall hard on your butt, you'll be grateful for that friendly hand lifting you back into the wild white you came here to see, hear, smell, touch, and taste.

This is Southern California's only cross-country skiing area.

Given the sporadic nature of snowfall at this elevation, when snow does appear, it's a one of a kind SoCal experience not to be missed. Photo courtesy of Kaitlin Chell. Picnic areas along the trail provide much needed rest spots for novice skiers, all while taking in the gorgeous views of the valley. Photo courtesy of Beverly Brown.

RIM NORDIC'S CROSS-COUNTRY TRAILS

WHAT Ten miles of groomed trails

WHERE 35050 State Hwy. 18, Running Springs (across the street from Snow Valley Mountain)

COST $20 for a full-day adult pass; $18 for equipment rental

PRO TIP If it's your first time cross-country skiing, even if you slope ski, choose the green trail. You'll appreciate the warm-up.

19 PICTURES HIDDEN AMONG THOUSANDS OF WORDS

How might pop culture promote education?

There are few places better built to engage all your senses than a space designed for children. What you find in the Children's Room at Corona Public Library will delight and surprise at every turn. Murals capture iconic images of California's unmatchable forests, mountains, and marine areas. Local history is represented by the historic homes along their famous "racetrack," lemon groves, and Heritage Park.

Brothers Sean and Patrick Johnson painstakingly researched each mural, putting the final touches on the collection in 2009. The two artists are better known today for their puppeteering talents through their company Swazzle, Inc., but it's obvious that a sense of fun and exploration runs through all their creative output. As a way to engage children of all ages, they included hidden figures in each mural. Many of these figures are inside jokes—depictions of library staff, whose research helped ensure an authentic representation, and their pets. But others are readily familiar to pop-culture consumers of any age.

Do you like Star Wars? Then you'll love these murals! The lemon groves feature a pair of TIE fighters zipping between branches, and you can relive the Jawas' capture of R2-D2 reimagined in the Eastern Sierras. The most difficult part to

CHILDREN'S ROOM AT CORONA PUBLIC LIBRARY

WHAT Panoramic California murals with hidden figures

WHERE 650 S Main St., Corona

COST Free

PRO TIP Want more than a mural of lemon groves? Visit Corona's Heritage Park for the real thing!

The first library in Corona started out as a small reading room in downtown's Gleason building, managed by the Women's Christian Temperance Union, in 1895. Photo courtesy of Larry Burns.

see may be the section inside the High Desert Room, a space for public meetings that also serves as the children's reading room. Ask the desk attendant if you can see the mural; if the room isn't in use, you might be able to take a peek. Cartoon buffs will appreciate how right it feels to see Wile E. Coyote chasing the Road Runner across the Mojave Desert.

Artists Sean and Patrick Johnson are known worldwide for their puppetry thanks to hits like *Avenue Q* and *Pee-wee's Playhouse.*

20 A POWERHOUSE TURNED ARTHOUSE

When function fails, does form fill the void?

This site is well-known around Norco, particularly by those who ride horses near the Santa Ana River. Just steps away from a main entrance into the city of Norco, it marks a period of fast growth and industrialization for the region.

THE ABANDONED PEDLEY POWERHOUSE

WHAT Two-story outdoor gallery for the creative arts

WHERE Near the corner of Crestview and North Drives, Pedley

COST Free

PRO TIP Walk the dirt access road about one-quarter mile to the building, which sits alongside a well-used riding trail. Once there, keep the area neat for others by leaving no trash and taking only photographs.

William Pedley founded the community that bears his name, as well as Riverside Power Company, in 1901. This plant was created to use the Santa Ana flow, via a six-mile feeder canal, to create power for the expanding Norco Valley.

But the operation was beset by problems both mechanical and financial. The power company folded in less than five years, whereas the plant limped along for several decades. Inconsistent water flow plus competing operations closed this facility as a power generator by the 1930s.

Lacking any other commercial function, the plant remained unused for decades. But it found new life starting in the '90s as an unofficial outdoor graffiti art gallery. There is little in the way of a coherent narrative to be discovered.

The upper floor has a colorful tapestry that uses a variety of pop-culture references and exaggerated forms, providing

While in operation, the powerhouse pulled water from the Santa Ana river through a six mile series of cement channels. Photo courtesy of Larry Burns.

a surrealistic experience once you crawl through the first-floor ceiling. There's a permanent ladder, but enter at your own risk—and even then, only in good weather and during daylight hours for your safety.

Part of the canal remains intact at the back of the property. Like the building, it has also been adorned with graffiti. The entire ad-hoc mural can be walked in just a few minutes.

Cities that successfully harnessed the power of their natural environment are the ones that continue to flourish to this day.

A MYSTERY WORTHY OF PERRY MASON

Are these the worlds' first tweets?

The Samuelson rocks are distinct, difficult to understand, and not easy to find. This qualifies them as quintessentially Inland Empire.

SAMUELSON'S ROCKS

WHAT Seven inscribed boulders on an old homestead

WHERE Quail Springs Day Use Lot, Joshua Tree National Park; take Quail Springs Trail, approximately five miles round trip.

COST $25 for a day-use park permit

PRO TIP Take a long lens to capture a few of the rocks, and their messages, placed high up on the hillside.

John Samuelson, born in Sweden, arrived in Joshua Tree in 1926, and a year later began to homestead with his wife, Margaret, in Lost Horse Canyon. He had some success in his prospecting and managed to lead a hardscrabble, but far from ordinary, existence. Although his years in the area were not many, they were marked by occasional differences with neighbors and law enforcement.

Samuelson occupied his free time carving messages into boulders strewn about the compound. The seven stones you'll find today cover all the subjects polite folk are taught to avoid: government, religion, politics, and the economy. The choice to carve his musings in stone fits the creative expressions evident in this area for thousands of years. Petroglyphs and

The thousands of abandoned mines of the desert speak to the pull of riches, starting with the gold rush in Northern California in 1848.

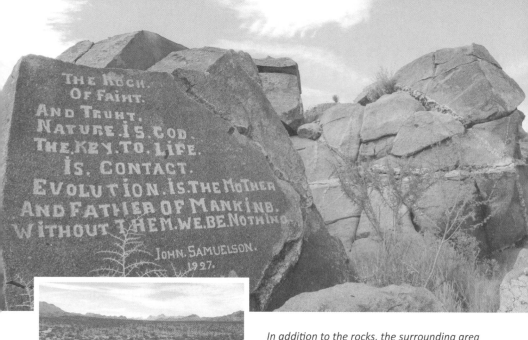

THE ROCK.
OF FAITH.
AND TRUHT.
NATURE IS GOD.
THE KEY TO LIFE.
IS. CONTACT.
EVOLUTION. IS THE MOTHER
AND FATHER OF MANKIND.
WITHOUT THEM. WE BE NOTHING.
JOHN. SAMUELSON.
1927.

WAKE UP
YOU TAX AND
BOND SLAVES
A POLITICIAN IS A BIRD
THAT GETS IN ON THE TAX
PAYERS POKET BOOK FOR A FAT
RAKE OF AND HIS FREE KEEPS.
HE LEADS YOU BY THE NOOSE
WITH ONE HAND WITH THE OTHER
HE DIGS IN YOUR POCKET
A FREIND OF THE BANKER AND BIG
BUSINESS WHY?.

In addition to the rocks, the surrounding area features other artifacts slowly rusting away. The Mojave Desert Land Trust (MDLT) protects this and dozens of other sites throughout the Mojave Desert. They protect more than 70,000 acres of prime desert habitat. Photos courtesy of Mojave Desert Land Trust.

pictographs are as plentiful in this desert as abandoned mine shafts. They all represent periods of rest and reflection between periods of difficult work. Clearly, Samuelson had plenty to reflect upon.

Much is known about him through his friendship with Erle Stanley Gardner, creator of the Perry Mason detective series. Samuelson hooked Gardner, a regular visitor to Joshua Tree, with wild tales of his passage to America, filled with kidnapping, shipwrecks, forbidden love, and giant ants protecting a vein of solid gold along the shores of Ghana.

Like Gardner, you may find yourself returning to this patch of desert more than once. The stories here attract, but the staying power lies in the beauty found naturally, then enhanced by the creative expressions of visionary artists.

POSTCARDS FROM BARSTOW

Are camels native to the Inland Empire?

Barstow has a long history as a transportation nexus. The murals by artist Kathy Fierro in this twenty-five-piece collection provide a beautiful visual field trip of regional history. Each mural has a small narrative attached, providing context and connection in many cases to modern-day Barstow. The most enjoyable aspect of these murals is the variety. So much is shared in such a small space. They must be seen to be fully appreciated.

The transportation history of this area dates all the way back to the Mojave Indians and their famous runners, who delivered messages and goods across unforgiving terrain. Those trails were later widened by the surveys of early settlers and the US government. In 1857, General Edward Beale used camels to traverse the route, finding them to be superior to mules in many respects. However, most were not as excited about the prospect, as the camels were thought to be ill-tempered beasts of burden, and they soon fell out of favor. Which is why the wagons that "won the west" were pulled by horses, donkeys, and mules. That also explains why there are thousands of these animals roaming the desert to this day.

Trains and automobiles are the preferred modes of transportation today, which

BARSTOW MURALS

WHAT Bright and informative displays of community heritage

WHERE Beale's Camel Mural, 200 N Second Ave., Barstow

COST Free

PRO TIP In December, the Desert Discovery Center's "Christmas Route 66 Tour" by horse drawn carriage is the best way to see it all at once.

In 1895, gold was discovered at Randsburg about 80 miles north of Barstow. It was one of the richest gold mining areas during the 20th century. The railroad and later Route 66 followed Beale's route. This mural was the combined effort of artists Kevin Varty, Jim Savoy, and Kathy Fierro and was completed in 2000. Photos courtesy of Larry Burns.

makes the nearby Barstow Depot one of the most popular places for a quick stop. When you visit, do more than just a quick stop. Drive a minute or two off the beaten path, then strap on a pair of walking shoes. Each of these murals holds secrets waiting for you to discover on your own.

The murals successfully connect the past to the present in a visually remarkable way.

23 A PEEK BEHIND THE CURTAIN OF THE DECORATIVE ARTS

See all the objects that transform a house into a home.

What's special about this historic home surrounded by sixteen acres of dazzling landscapes and horticultural wonder? Without a doubt, there's no better place to experience the decorative arts. Starting with the sixteenth century, this museum recognizes the impact that a curated personal space can achieve.

The museum was created and donated to the community by Edward Eberle and Dean Stout. The pair built this home to house their burgeoning collection, to buy and sell antiques, and to create a permanent place for this art form.

The decorative arts, broadly, are the items that give a room or a home a sense of identity. True to that purpose, the collection is spread across several themed rooms, and each item inside was carefully selected to evoke an emotion or capture the values (and material wealth) of a particular period.

The collection provides high-quality examples across three centuries and touches nearly every continent. The works here represent a lifetime of collecting. What is curated here

THE EDWARD-DEAN MUSEUM AND GARDENS

WHAT Two Men. One Vision. Thousands of artifacts.

WHERE 9401 Oak Glen Rd., Cherry Valley

COST $5 for adults; free for children under twelve and veterans with IDs

PRO TIP Led by the friendly, knowledgeable staff, the tour is a bargain and highly recommended. Hours: Thursday–Saturday, 10 a.m.–5 p.m.

The museum sits within 16 acres of gardens and natural habitat, complementing the beauty of the surrounding Cherry Valley. Photo courtesy of Edward-Dean Museum.

are demonstrations of the tastes and habits of those who lived in Southern California during the middle to late twentieth century. The furniture, wall hangings, accessories, and architectural flourishes demonstrate what matters in an artistic scene that is constantly evolving.

Bibliophiles can spend hours poring over copies of classic architectural texts, such as a copy of *The Architecture of A. Palladio*. The book heavily influenced Thomas Jefferson's design of Monticello and the University of Virginia. A second Founding Father literary artifact is a complete copy of George Washington's handwritten account ledger for Mount Vernon. The Library of Congress created these commemorative copies near the fiftieth anniversary of the first president's death.

One hallmark of the decorative arts is its ability to use functional objects and limited space to evoke an emotional response.

A STRUCTURE AND A STATUE INSPIRED BY NATIVE AMERICAN CULTURE

What kind of refuge might empathy and attention to beauty provide?

Here you will find two examples of art inspired by Native American tribes. Cabot Yerxa, a lifetime collector and advocate for the preservation and redevelopment of Indian culture, was the genius behind the museum. The pueblo itself was a Hopi Indian–inspired creation.

The four-story, five-thousand-square-foot dwelling was created with the long-term plan to convert it into a museum to both share the Native American artifacts with the world and continue educating in the arena of Indian rights and culture. Most of the raw materials were salvaged from nearby structures, including Yerxa's original 1925 homestead.

Passion attracts passion, and great talent seeks out its equal. Be sure to spend time admiring another artist with a similar lifelong passion for Native American culture. Peter "Wolf" Toth is a Cold War–era immigrant to the US who fled Hungary at age eleven. He saw parallels between his own harrowing refugee experience and the long struggle of Native American Indians for human rights and equality.

The nearly forty-foot and forty-five-ton Indian head sculpture, titled *Waokiye*, is just one of seventy-three in Toth's North American collection called the "Trail of the Whispering Giants." *Waokiye* is the only piece in the collection you can see in California. The feather came from incense cedar collected in nearby Idyllwild, and the head was carved from a single

Filled with Native American art and artifacts, souvenirs of Cabot's travels around the world, displays on Native American Rights, and Cabot's own works of art, the Pueblo Museum officially opened to the public in 1949. Photo courtesy of Larry Burns.

sequoia log. In 2009, Toth returned for several months to touch up the monument, adding details to represent the Agua Caliente Indians.

Together, these two larger-than-life artifacts capture the many influences and values of this varied region of California. Both represent a lifetime of work on the part of artists, created to honor the sacrifices and accomplishments of people who came before them. In their examples, visitors can witness what is possible when a single person sets out to make their community a better place through thoughtful conservation and creative expression.

CABOT'S PUEBLO MUSEUM AND TOTH'S WOODEN INDIAN HEAD

WHAT An enclave of art and history

WHERE 67616 Desert View Ave., Desert Hot Springs

COST $13 for the museum; free access to the outdoor areas and gift shop

PRO TIP This is an ideal place to rest and refresh in your desert travels. The outdoor area includes wonderfully appointed restrooms and clean drinking fountains. Hours: Tuesday–Sunday, 9 a.m.–4 p.m.; 9 a.m.–1 p.m. in summer.

This is the only place in California to see an example of the North American "Trail of the Whispering Giants" created by Peter "Wolf" Toth.

25 A STUDY IN REJECTING AUTHORITY AND EMBRACING CREATIVE HUMAN EXPRESSION

Does anything fill the void better than art?

Full disclosure: East Jesus, the only outdoor museum that's part of the Imperial County Museum Association, is not in the Inland Empire proper. One of the favorite pastimes of residents is to debate what is and what isn't part of the Inland Empire. Sometimes, we find ourselves excluding a group. Other times, groups that are in the IE don't really want to be in the IE! But this is a diverse, inclusive family. We don't care who your momma is; if you think like us, you're part of the family.

One visit and you'll understand why East Jesus belongs in the Inland Empire. And to play along with the theme of "empire," it would behoove any empire worth its salt to find places to expand. If the IE truly became a conquering nation, the tip of that spear might

EAST JESUS

WHAT An improbably improvised community on the edge of the world

WHERE East Jesus Rd., Niland

COST Free

PRO TIP For your safety, visit only during daylight hours. Roads and residences are sometimes poorly lit—but are well-guarded. This community welcomes you, but they do not suffer fools.

This is the only museum in the US that features a clothing-optional shooting range.

Fans of outdoor art come from all walks of life, evidenced by the variety of guests that frequent it's galleries. Photo courtesy of Larry Burns.

point south and east, to East Jesus. And if you're already in Mecca for the International Banana Museum, you might as well drive the extra thirty minutes east and discover some one-of-a-kind finds.

East Jesus, which has permanent collections as well as rotation exhibits, welcomes and supports all art forms. But the museum shines in the areas of giant outdoor assemblage that can overwhelm the senses with size, skill, and cultural references. Some of the art seen at the annual Burning Man Festival is displayed here during the off season. And the interactive pirate ship, one among several interactive exhibits, will have kids and adults alike scrambling aboard and shouting hearty "ahoys" in no time flat.

The museum, which has no admission fee, greatly appreciates donations of art supplies, building materials, and staples such as water, canned goods, and fresh fruit for the community. Before you visit, check the museum's website (www.eastjesus.org) for currently needed items.

26 A HEALTHY SNACK ALONG YOUR BUSY COMMUTE

The fulfilment of an artist's vision?

The Inland Empire is no stranger to the occasional piece of inspired roadside art. Sure, there are dozens of worthy roadside rock formations to choose from. But what's distinctly special here is how the artist has used the natural layout of the rocks to create something inspired. Further, its continued "shine" demonstrates the do-it-together tastes of the Inland Empire.

The apple has no connection to the Inland Empire. Some places grow them, but citrus has been the groove here for well over a century. What you see here is artist inspiration at its folksy finest. Neil Larson lived near this formation, and he finally could no longer resist the impulse to paint them up. Looking at Larson's creation, one can't help but see the apple sliced up and ready to share with a couple of kids over lunch. So, credit to Larson for seeing

NEIL LARSON'S APPLE FOLK ART

WHAT A "slice" of Inland Empire folk art

WHERE Intersection of 27665 Hwy. 74 with Wasson Canyon Road, Perris

COST Free

PRO TIP Join a secret society by eating an apple on the site and leaving the core.

Roadside folk art has a vibe all its own. Despite its outlaw appearance, it's often maintained by passionate local volunteers.

The boulders sit along a key Inland road. It is known as the Ortega Highway from San Juan Capistrano to Lake Elsinore. It is the Pines to Palms Highway in the San Jacinto Mountains. Photo courtesy of Larry Burns.

something, then making an artistic statement that lets the rest of us appreciate his perspective as well.

The community spirit of the Inland Empire truly shines in Larson's work. He saw something whimsical, painted it, and eventually moved away. Fans of outdoor art then took it upon themselves to maintain this place and adopted the sliced apple as their own. Every few years, a fresh coat of paint is applied. No word yet on what color the apple will be next.

WATER PARK GONE GRAFFITI ART ENCLAVE

What springs to life when the water runs dry?

There are two kinds of history in the Inland Empire: short lived and long lived. Both are exciting to learn about, and both tell important stories about the IE. While conditions vary, the peoples and things that last are those that have regular access to water, the single most valuable resource we've got.

This water park was part of a drive in the late 1950s and early 1960s to put the community on the map, and it did so with stunning success. Sitting alongside busy Interstate 15, the main artery for anyone in Southern California making a weekend trek to Las Vegas, the water park provided weary road warriors a respite from the dusty trail.

Opened to the public in 1962, Lake Dolores Waterpark was a day-trip destination for residents across Southern California. A tourist mainstay up through the 1980s, it was closed as people found other ways to spend their entertainment dollars. Then, it was rebranded as Rock a-Hoola

LAKE DOLORES WATER PARK

WHAT A graffiti cathedral that was once a water-themed amusement park

WHERE Exit 206 on Interstate 15, along Western Frontage Road (Hacienda Road)

COST Free

PRO TIP Use care during your visit as the site is not regularly maintained.

Originally designed by Bob Byer as a private family retreat, "Lake Dolores Water Park" was America's first water park when it debuted in 1962.

People often wonder how the 270 acre Lake Dolores was filled in the desert. The answer lies below, from the Mojave Aquifer. In 2013, TrustoCorp, a group of artists from New York City, transformed the park into a "TrustoLand" as an artistic statement, by repainting many signs and buildings with unusual images and messages. Photos courtesy of Larry Burns.

and reopened in the late 1990s. But an expensive worker's compensation lawsuit contributed to the water park's permanent demise a few years later. Between incarnations, indie band The Friendly Indians released a 1996 album, "Greetings … from Lake Dolores," with cover art showing the water slides in all their glory.

Today, it's been adopted by hipsters and graffiti artists. Some may recognize parts of the park in advertisements, as several commercials and TV shows have been filmed here in the decades since its closure. Like a desert mirage, new water park plans appear on the horizon every few years but have yet to materialize.

28 ASSEMBLAGE SCULPTURES IN AN OPEN-AIR DESERT MUSEUM

What better way is there to discover the desert's secrets than through the work of its artists?

The deserts of the Inland Empire are not the empty wastelands people sometimes see from the outside. Those who live here know that life abounds in the desert; unique species of birds, plants, reptiles, mammals, and fish call this place home.

This is also the adopted home of many artists—so many that another book could be written just on the secret artists of this part of California. One artist who represents the spirit of this region and, specifically, the purposes and values of assemblage sculpture is Noah Purifoy.

Driving up to the grounds of this outdoor museum can be disorienting. Perhaps it's the bumpy, quarter-mile dirt road at the entrance. More likely, it's the space itself. Purifoy's work seems to dominate and shrink within the landscape as you approach.

These large sculptures, which sit within a ten-acre museum space, defy easy understanding. Some of them seem to be imitating the forms of the desert. Others, in particular the sculptured buildings, provide an eerie mirror of the abandoned

NOAH PURIFOY'S OUTDOOR DESERT ART MUSEUM

WHAT A collection of Noah Purifoy's work from 1989 to 2004

WHERE 63030 Blair Ln., Joshua Tree

COST Free

PRO TIP Rainy weather can make the road to the museum inaccessible for several days at a time, so plan accordingly.

The last fifteen years of Purifoy's prolific career were spent filling up this ten-acre outdoor museum. Constructed entirely from junked materials, this otherworldly environment is one of California's great art historical wonders. Photo courtesy of Noah Purifoy Foundation.

and near-abandoned places that dot the desert. All of them capture the pace, purpose, and raw materials that provide the special character of the Inland deserts.

Noah Purifoy's work is in the permanent collection of several notable museums around the country. But this is the only place where you can experience the genius of his work 365 days a year. The Noah Purifoy Foundation, which manages day-to-day operations here, hosts guided tours during the foundation's annual fundraising activities and by advance appointment at the foundations's website (www.noahpurifoy.com).

"I hope my work provides inspiration for a person to do today what they couldn't do yesterday, no matter what it is. That's art. That's the fundamental creative process and it's something that changes people and empowers them." —Noah Purifoy

29 A TREE GROWS IN [THE DESERT]

What do you build when you have everything you need?

People are at once surprised and proud of the interest shown toward the artistic creations and havens built out of nothing, often discarded "nothings." There's very little fanfare surrounding this special Inland Empire site. In a nutshell, a man named Elmer, who has been collecting bottles for years, puts them together in fun little displays and opens his property to the public when he feels like it. Fortunately, he feels like sharing his work and talking about art and the purpose behind these creations just about every day. If the gate is open, stroll on inside.

The self-sufficient operation has been open nearly every day since 2000. The use of reclaimed material fits this folk art funhouse. Elmer doesn't consider himself an artist, nor would he classify his creations as "folk art." In fact, he seems to eschew labels of nearly any kind.

The tradition of finding treasure in the trash heaps of the past was started by Elmer's

ELMER'S BOTTLE TREE RANCH

WHAT Outdoor exhibit starring thousands of glass bottles

WHERE 24266 National Trails Hwy., Oro Grande

COST Free; donations dropped in the wishing well appreciated

PRO TIP If you run into Elmer during your visit, strike up a conversation and hang out a spell. He sometimes shares what he knows about other secret desert spots.

The driving philosophy of the creator, and this place, is simple: Do what you like.

58

The Bottle Tree Ranch is Elmer's home. There are no official hours, but if you stop by in the daytime on a weekday or weekend and the gates are open, you can go ahead and walk around among the bottle trees--you might even bump into Elmer! Everything you see here was found in the surrounding area.

According to Elmer, the desert contains thousands of other valuable artifacts just waiting to be uncovered. Photos courtesy of Larry Burns.

father. The bottles came from a long-abandoned town called Providence. It was Elmer, however, who had the inspiration to take the bottles from storage and hang them up in all their shining glory. A walk through these groves provides smiles and moments of wonder around every turn. These glass and metal sculptures exemplify the necessity and the joy uncovered through recycling and reuse.

One thing that will strike you about this place is the hospitality. It mirrors the sustaining values that were part of these places for nearly as long as there have been human populations in the Inland Empire.

WRITER'S BLOCK

You've just read four hundred books of poetry, now what?

Few items entice quite like free, which is why the Garcia Center for the Arts intends to give away most of its materials, time, and resources. Actually, the hope is to inspire others and make San Bernardino a shining example of how a community of arts cultivates peace and prosperity. How all the books arrived here is another Inland Empire story of responsible reuse.

Few bibliophiles would recycle a book, but reuse is another idea altogether. And reuse was the inspiration of Nikia Chaney, a local poet, professor, and Inlandia's Literary Laureate from 2016 to 2018. In addition to these accomplishments, she worked as a screener for the Kingsley and Kate Tufts Poetry Awards through Claremont Graduate University. With that job done, Chaney wondered how to make good use of the four hundred books she'd screened and now overflowed the shelves of her home library. The best way to get the works into people's hands, she reasoned, was to create a totally free poetry library, in partnership with Inlandia Institute and the Garcia Center for the Arts.

The checking in and out process hearkens back to a predigital world; it may even predate card catalogs! It's all on the honor system, with checking books in or out available only during regular operating hours. First, you grab a "book mark" or two;

INLANDIA POETRY LIBRARY

WHAT Modern poetry by a diverse pool of award hopefuls

WHERE 536 W 11th St., San Bernardino.

COST Free

PRO TIP Hours: Tuesday–Thursday and Saturday, 9 a.m.–12 p.m. Consult the Center's events calendar (www.sbvca.org/calendar) for weekly programs and special events.

This 400 volume collection is one of the largest examples of literary reuse projects found in Southern California. In addition to poetry, the library space provides dozens of books on local and national art, history, and culture. Photos courtesy of Larry Burns.

they're basically long, flat pieces of finished wood. When you remove a book from the shelf, you put the mark in its place to ensure the book you borrow is returned to the proper spot.

And when do you return the book? Whenever you want. There are no late fees at this library. What a wonderful way to introduce folks to poetry and the vital role that libraries play in our lives!

Along with fostering a love of poetry, this space regularly hosts plays, opera, orchestras and other live music, and more!

31 THE ARTISTRY OF EVERYDAY OBJECTS

When is a chair more than just a chair?

Born to Lebanese immigrants in the small dairy farming community of Chino, Sam Maloof gained fame worldwide as one of the greatest craftsmen in woodworking. During the mid-twentieth century, an eager cadre of artists and craftspersons were drawn to the Pomona Valley by nearby Scripps College.

These artists of all stripes shared and collaborated over the decades, helping each other with projects and sometimes trading their art to each other in exchange for services.

The original site of the Maloof home and woodworking shop was nestled 3.5 miles south of the current location, in a gorgeous little lemon grove. But today, six lanes of traffic speed along Interstate 210 at the original location. Relocating this historic home instead of changing the freeway's planned route saved about 120 homes, occupied by Maloof's neighbors, from eminent domain.

Fortunately, Maloof was there to make sure every plank, every post, and every brick was properly placed. No detail was overlooked in the resettlement. The orientation of the buildings and their distance from one another was replicated to within a foot! The newer buildings on the site contain training facilities and related functions.

THE MALOOF HOME

WHAT Original home and workshop, along with new galleries and educational facilities

WHERE 5131 Carnelian St., Alta Loma

COST $15 and up for home tours, with discounts for seniors, children, and the military; free self-guided tours of the grounds

PRO TIP When you visit, be sure to make time to visit the Pyramid Room, a fine-arts exhibition space highlighting environmental stewardship and community building. Hours: Thursday and Saturday, 12–4 p.m.

Despite the waiting lists that developed for his pieces, his dedication to handcrafting each item meant that his output was small; no more than 100 pieces were produced annually. Maloof was described by the Smithsonian Institution as "America's most renowned contemporary furniture craftsman" and People magazine dubbed him "The Hemingway of Hardwood." Photos courtesy of Larry Burns.

Maloof believed that life was beautiful if you made it beautiful. He also believed in using the materials at hand to create the beauty you wanted in the world. His home is made of redwood, an abundant product in California after World War II. The red brick floors connect you to the earth, keep things cool, and are easily replaced when they crack. He used cheap, readily available bridge washers to hold much of it together.

Sam Maloof was the first craftsperson honored with a MacArthur "Genius Grant" in 1985, but his business card always read "woodworker." In all areas, he managed to combine form and function in a way that made his creations appear common and priceless at the same time. It's the way many feel about Maloof to this day, and it personifies the spirit and ethics of the Inland Empire.

Five-year lead times were the norm for Maloof's furniture, with one reasonable exception: every baby crib was a rush delivery!

COVE ARTISTS' COLONY AT CATHEDRAL CITY

Colonies provide crucial social support to those who think and live outside the box.

This part of Southern California is dotted with hermitages and places of refuge, most centered around artistic endeavors. For as long as there has been western civilization in the west, there has been a nearly constant movement in the opposite direction, toward places offering an escape from modernity.

Artists moved to the desert to escape commercial as well as social influences on their art. California was especially welcoming to alternative lifestyles and utopian ideals, and colonies provided places for like-minded artists to meet. It's a cycle that continues to this day. Many of the IE's special little corners came about through the hopes and dreams expressed by artists and entrepreneurs alike.

Agnes Pelton—who used this part of the Inland Empire to perfect her plein air landscapes of the desert—is the most widely known person associated with the Cathedral City Cove artist's colony. In later years, her work became more abstract and transcendental in nature, likely due to other influences in the area, from spiritualists to fellow artists.

Pelton shared paints, ideas, and a love of the desert landscape with other notables, such as Cornelia Sussman, Matille Seaman, Mary Price, Harriet Day, and Emma Christina Lillian. Lillian arrived as a thirty-five-year-old former wardrobe

---

The entrance of this house used to open onto "E" Street. But as the community grew, the entrance was moved to the "F" Street side.

From the 1930's to the 1950's, this vibrant artists colony was visited by world renown writers, painters, and musicians, who came to visit, teach, and create. Photo courtesy of Larry Burns.

AGNES PELTON HOUSE

WHAT Historical homes and artwork from one of the Inland Empire's oldest art colonies

WHERE 68688 "F" St., Cathedral City

COST Free; $20 for the annual spring tour

PRO TIP Park on nearby Cathedral Canyon Drive and walk in to avoid blocking the alley artwork and traffic along the narrow streets.

designer for Hollywood film stars. Each of them found something that gave their lives and their art new purpose and significance. In addition to providing support to one another, their efforts created the Coachella Valley's first art gallery, the Desert Art Center, in 1954.

The Agnes Pelton House is the star attraction along this well-preserved part of history. Lining the alley running between "E" and "F" Streets, you'll find several pieces of art to appreciate year-round. The works of many of the artists from the colony are featured, as well as the talents of current artists who continue the colony tradition of historical preservation and innovative creativity.

33 A PILGRIMAGE FOR CARTOONISTS

Did you know the saguaro cactus only grows in the Sonoran desert?

Artists have been inspired by the landscapes of the Inland Empire for millennia. One famous artist inspired by his IE childhood was Charles Schulz, creator of the comic strip "Peanuts." The strip continues to be printed in hundreds of newspapers, even though a new "Peanuts" hasn't been written since early 2000. That speaks to the popularity and strong connection that the strip created with its readers.

Spike is more than Snoopy's less famous brother. He was a real dog that Schultz loved during his boyhood in Needles. The antics of that wild pup would serve as foundational elements for the character Snoopy. And although the Schulz family stayed only a year, returning in 1930 to Minnesota, the place clearly left a mark on the budding artist.

Spike made occasional appearances in the strip and the cartoon specials throughout the years. He was rarely without his fedora; his best bud, a saguaro cactus; and a dry line about the state of things.

The saguaro cactus, often appearing alongside Spike in the comic strips, can be found in the nearby Whipple Mountains to the south of Needles. Photo courtesy of Gloria Rohrer.

WHAT Unique "Peanuts" memorabilia at the northeastern edge of the Inland Empire

WHERE 2451 Needles Hwy., Needles

COST Free

PRO TIP This Subway location is open 24/7, so it's never a bad time to drop by for a "howdy" to Spike.

Needles was a childhood home to Schulz around 1930 where he attended D Street School, now Katie Hohstadt Elementary. Photo courtesy of Gloria Rohrer.

Local booster and Snoopy fan Joe Jones received formal permission from Charles M. Schulz Creative Associates, the organization that oversees the commercial aspects of Schulz's estate, to erect a Spike statue. In addition to its blessing, the organization sent along a few framed copies of the strip to commemorate this special marker.

The statue, which debuted at the Needles Chamber of Commerce, is currently displayed inside the local Subway restaurant. Not what you might expect inside a Subway, but one of the promises of the Inland Empire is that it will deliver plenty of unexpected fun and joy—no matter where the road may take you.

Schulz's childhood dog, Spike, was the inspiration for Snoopy.

34 A PLACE FOR TOSSED-ASIDE TOYS TO FINALLY BE THEMSELVES

Didn't you know that being small is the be-all?

Sunvale Village is the whimsical invention of artist Cathy Allen, whose creative work spans several genres. Her use of recycled materials, natural materials, and the "outdoors as canvas" eliminates the boundary between *Sunvale Village* and the real world. Her dedication to using junked materials—every strip of material was salvaged from illegal dump sites or discards around the desert—is an environmental choice.

This quasi-permanent installation (wind and rain cause regular reimagining) works as a lens through which to understand our very real human emotions and actions. This curated five acres of creosote brush, bursage, mesquite, and cactus intentionally blurs the line between where you live and where art lives. Each little, right-sized, home—as of 2018, there were over thirty—is a stand-alone diorama that investigates contemporary American issues and ideas through puns, art shout-outs, and pop-culture references.

The "residents" come from all walks of life, and their stories reflect many of the real reasons people live in the desert. A few are burned-out entertainers seeking peace and quiet. Others

---

SUNVALE VILLAGE: A COMMUNITY FOR THE SMALL

WHAT Refuge for things others consider refuse

WHERE 79098 Sunvale Rd., Wonder Valley

COST Free tours by appointment

PRO TIP Connect and follow their goings-on virtually at the Sunvale Village Facebook page.

The site-specific installation of Sunvale Village is a playful commentary on significant contemporary issues such as the environment, gentrification of communities and ownership, and politics. Individual sculptural pieces are assembled mixed media junk, with all materials scavenged from abandoned refuse or illegal dump sites. Photo courtesy of Larry Burns.

hope the open spaces and like-minded friends will help them shake off their cynicism. Some are refugees. All of them stay because the desert landscape gives life to the peoples and ideas that embrace its limitations. It also has a well-trained, conscientious group of volunteers called the Sentinels, who keep the community safe from the larger world and its selfish "big ideas."

At the visitor center—which serves as an office, studio, and waystation for future residents of the installation—you can pick up the latest property map. You'll need one, plus a guide, to explain the what and why of each home. You can catch up on the latest local news because unlike many human communities, this one has its own newspaper, *The Wee Web Post-it Sunvale Village News.*

Many come to the desert with the mistaken idea that the landscape is barren, empty of life or anything interesting. They arrive to transform it, or take from it, or make it their own. This installation, and the people living here, say otherwise.

The desert can play with your sense of self. Here, artistic play is used to identify and define purpose.

35 STAR-CROSSED LOVERS MEMORIALIZED

What lines are you willing to cross for love?

Stories are a way to share a history and to make a difference. When Helen Hunt Jackson published her fictional love story set in the Hemet-San Jacinto area, she hoped to capture the hopes and dreams that made this place. Specifically, she hoped to bring attention to the plight of Native Americans struggling to survive ever-increasing waves of interstate migration. Water disputes, disease, war, and forced resettlements played largely on her mind while she travelled the area and wrote.

Jackson was partially successful. Her new tale, the Inland Empires's version of *Romeo and Juliet*, sparked interest well beyond the border and was an immediate bestseller. Ramona prompted a flurry of home and infrastructure building to support tourists flocking in to walk around the "real life" setting for Ramona and Alessandro's tragic love affair.

The general plot accurately depicts the social and economic barriers of the time. In the mid-1800s, following California's statehood in 1850, land was transferred from several Californio-owned rancheros into the hands of new Americans. *Ramona*, published in 1884, told the story of a half-Indian servant of an aging Californio family who was being forced into an arranged marriage to the oldest son. Fate, however,

---

RAMONA: THE TALE OF RAMONA AND ALESSANDRO

WHAT America's longest-running outdoor drama

WHERE 27400 Ramona Bowl Rd.

COST $5 for parking; $20 and up for show tickets.

PRO TIP The annual show is staged every April. See it free by volunteering to act in a background role.

Ramona Bowl
Home of The Ramona Outdoor Play

In outdoor drama, the setting is a key part of the presentation. In many ways, the Ramona Bowl is as important a part of the play as the costumes or the props. It lends a sense of realism to the show, and help to immerse the audience in the story. Woven into the romance of Ramona and Alessandro is a glimpse of the tragic history of Southern California's native people. It is a love story with a moral, a message that is as important today as it was when the story of Ramona was written more than a century ago. Photos courtesy of Larry Burns.

intervenes, bringing Ramona to the attention of an Indian shepherd named Alessandro. In a story older than Shakespeare, the two fall in love and fail in their escape. Death closes in.

But the story lives! In 1923, a yearly outdoor pageant celebrating *Ramona* was inaugurated in a natural amphitheater just outside the city. In its heyday, its message of love and the tragic lives of the Mission Indians attracted upwards of eighty thousand people. Thanks to its timeless message, it's now the longest-running outdoor drama staged anywhere in the United States.

Helen Hunt Jackson was a pen pal of another famous American literary giant, poet Emily Dickinson.

36 A PLACE FOR [YOUR] STUFF

Ever wonder where to get a vintage 1925 window crank?

It's not easy keeping secrets in a city this big, but that's exactly what Peter J. Weber accomplished in Riverside. Before turning his skills to this one-of-a-kind blend of art deco, art nouveau, craftsman, and Moorish influences, Weber was the chief designer at the firm responsible for the International Rotunda at the Mission Inn, as well as several projects that established the mission revival style of architecture as a unique Southern California contribution nearly a century ago.

Today, Weber's most interesting creation hides in the shadow of a chain hotel.

It serves as an informal Home Depot for your turn-of-the-century craftsman. The current curator of the home, Peter Weber, the last surviving member of the Weber clan, opens the home for visitors from time to time. Not to worry if you arrive when it is closed. The exterior is worth a visit and a few pictures. But to see all the house has to offer, visit when it's guaranteed to be open: during the Old Riverside Foundation's annual Vintage Home Tour in the spring. You'll be able to talk with Weber himself, as well as leaders in local history, arts, and architecture.

Peter J. Weber was chief designer for the architectural firm of G. Stanley Wilson. Mr. Weber applied his talents to the International Rotunda at the Mission Inn, Redlands Post Office, and many other Wilson projects. The Weber house is listed in the National Register of Historic Places and is recognized locally as Riverside City Landmark #52. It also serves as the HQ for the Old Riverside Foundation. Photos courtesy of Larry Burns.

The Inland Empire's eastern desert has some of the largest solar projects in the United States. Those modern developments connect to a long history of energy innovation and conservation. The Weber home was built using recycled material. How did its exterior brick, displaying just the right amount of wear, come to be? It was repurposed from the citrus packing houses—as was some of the wood, which is unique with its many handcrafted features. This early twentieth-century creation even has a solar water heater whose collector panels were once windshields.

This structure pioneered green building and LEED (Leadership in Energy and Environmental Design) construction practices before the practice had a formal name.

37

WHITE LINES

How did a white dividing line become standard practice on highways?

The Inland Empire has one of the most acute doctor shortages in the country, a situation that has long existed. So Indio was particularly happy to see June McCarroll, MD, arrive in the early part of the nineteenth century. After a distinguished medical career, she followed her husband here, apparently intending to be a prairie wife and little more. But the acute need for physicians—particularly by the very poorest, who worked in the fields and had little access to modern conveniences—prompted her to jump in to help.

DR JUNE MCCONNELL HISTORICAL MARKER

WHAT Another example of the failure of "mansplaining"

WHERE Intersection of Indio Boulevard and Fargo Street, Indio

COST Free

PRO TIP Minutes away, the stretch of Interstate 10 near exit 144 (Golf Center Parkway) is officially named the "Dr. June McConnell Memorial Highway."

To provide care to those in need, she took to driving around the desert, her six-shooter and surgeon's tools ever at her side. And that's how she found herself one night on a dark stretch of highway, facing a freight truck barreling down the center of Indio Boulevard. Forced off the road, she sustained minor injuries that gave rise to a lingering question: How can we prevent head-on collisions?

This clever medical doctor's solution was simple and direct, which describes the kind of

The good doctor also established Indio's first library, so tuberculosis patients would have reading materials, in 1907.

On April 24, 2002, to honor her contribution to road safety, California officially designated the stretch of Interstate 10 near Indio east of the Indio Boulevard/Jefferson Street exit as "The Doctor June McCarroll Memorial Freeway." As one of the only physicians around the Imperial and Coachella Valleys, she provided care to tens of thousands of Cahuilla Indians during her tenure. Photos courtesy of Larry Burns.

medicine she became famous for: What about painting a white line down the center of the highway so everyone knows where to drive? Those in power didn't appreciate her vision. The local chamber and board of supervisors heard, and quickly rejected, this woman's advice.

But she persisted, leaving that meeting and immediately painting a mile of Indio herself—by hand, at night. A campaign began, catching the attention of the newly formed California Highway Commission. The commissioners loved the idea and in 1917 formalized the center white line as the state's standard road design. As is often the case with ideas initiated in California, the world adopted the practice soon after.

38

AN ALLERGY-FREE WAY TO "TIPTOE THROUGH THE TULIPS"

How might we best document the effects of pollution and climate change?

In terms of the size and scope of the University of California Riverside's collection, you'd be hard pressed to find a better catalog of vascular plant and lichen specimens anywhere else in the world. Given the diverse geological features of the two-county region (San Bernardino and Riverside), it's no surprise that nearly half of the more than three hundred thousand specimens in UCR's extensive archives were found in Southern California.

This immense collection contains specimens from every state in Mexico and all but one state in the US. While most of the world is familiar with the area's iconic Joshua Tree, thanks to U2's debut album, much of the varied fauna can go unnoticed.

One of those finds went unnoticed, or at least undocumented, until 2009. Curators Andy Sanders and Mitch Provance were part of the team that identified, sampled, and analyzed a spectacular specimen of Palmer's oak, aka the "Jurupa oak," that started life in the Pleistocene era. It's at least thirteen thousand years old, by far the oldest living thing in California. In fact, it's one of the oldest living things in the world.

Scientists at this single location identify thousands of species annually.

Most items in the collections were generated locally in relatively recent times, providing the best current pictures of the flora of Southern California. The UCR Herbarium documents the abundance and distribution of species, including changes in range over time and the arrival of invasive species, the rediscovery of "extinct" species, and the collapse of native plant populations regionally. Photos courtesy of Larry Burns.

UNIVERSITY OF CALIFORNIA RIVERSIDE HERBARIUM

WHAT An unmatched collection of the Inland Empire's diverse natural environment.

WHERE 900 University Ave. (SW corner of UCR's campus), Riverside

COST $5 for parking

PRO TIP Time permitting, ask a scientist to show you the "artisanal" specimen pressing tools. Then build your own at home.

Scientists and amateurs alike have relied on this free hidden resource for decades. Every year, hundreds bring in for identification the plant samples they've discovered on a hike or that have popped up between their azaleas.

When you make it to campus to check out that sample or ask a question only a scientist would appreciate, be sure to fully explore all the campus has to offer. UCR is a center for agricultural innovation, and its botanic garden has thousands of identified species. You'll find excellent examples of native species carefully placed at nearly every turn of this research institution.

39 NASA'S INTERSTELLAR SWITCHBOARD

Hello Major Tom. Are you receiving?

The Goldstone Deep Space Complex is a NASA-operated communications center. Those first photos of Mars? Those first static-filled messages as humans set foot on the moon for the first time in 1969? They all came through the Inland Empire, home of the Deep Space Network's (DSN) first installation in the world.

This is a special place—one of only three on earth; you'll need to grab a passport and head to Spain or Australia for the others. It's also special because it provides communication links to the humans and probes satellites flying invisibly across the skies day and night. It never sleeps, and it never rests in its quest to answer our questions about the universe. Goldstone connects us and our equipment across the solar system, giving us unprecedented ways to experience our place in the world.

GOLDSTONE DEEP SPACE COMPLEX VISITOR'S CENTER

WHAT Interactive learning center for space exploration

WHERE Inside the Harvey House, 681 N First Ave., Barstow

COST Free

PRO TIP Try to visit when NASA's Mars Roadshow is in town so you can witness the cutting edge of space exploration. Hours: Monday–Friday, 9 a.m.–4 p.m.; Saturday, 10 a.m.–2 p.m.

As part of the Deep Space Network, they are the Google of space communications. They control it all!

From the first planetary encounters, the first human landing on the moon, to missions that reach the farthest points in our solar system, the Goldstone Deep Space Communications Complex has been there to bring home the critical data, images, or science. Goldstone began its operations for NASA by tracking the Pioneer probes to the Moon. Photos courtesy of Larry Burns.

It also connects to regional history: Goldstone was the name of the abandoned mining town predating this development. The complex is a study in contrast. It's a remote desert area designed to house the technology and innovative practices that will lift mankind off this planet and someday provide the link between here and our first human outpost on another orb.

The sensitive nature of the equipment limits public access to the antennas themselves. But the Visitor's Center, which captures the magic and the science of what it's all about, is waiting for you! Listen to actual space recordings, explore early modes of space transport, picture yourself as an astronaut, and learn more about how the IE is shaping the final frontier. You'll be able to immerse yourself in spectacular space oddities for decades to come.

40 OH, GIVE ME A HOME WHERE THE [DONKEY] ROAM

Is the donkey native to SoCal?

Beasts of burden transformed the West. However, after they were no longer needed, they were sometimes turned out into the wilderness. That may explain how these donkeys and burros came to Reche Canyon and the surrounding community.

You may wonder who cares for these wild animals. Over time, an interesting mix of private and public resources has joined forces to help keep both people and the donkeys healthy and safe. In 2008, new state laws were passed to make it easier for local agencies to offer aid to the three hundred or so wild burros and donkeys that call this patch of the IE their permanent home.

On the private side, DonkeyLand is a 501(c)(3) nonprofit charitable organization, started by Amber LaVonne and her family. Their story epitomizes IE problem-solving in all its seat-of-your-pants glory. How dedicated must a person be to care for a young or sick donkey? Consider the fact that a young donkey without a mother still needs to feed about every hour, and you can see the toll that caring for one animal can take. Local donors, as well as famous folks like Bob Barker, longtime animal activist

Donkeys use a series of natural and human-made corridors to find food, water, and shelter in and around Reche Canyon. They are known to eat wild grasses (and a few lawns), flowers, bushes, and weeds. Photo courtesy of Riverside County Animal Services.

and host of *The Price Is Right*, ensure that abandoned and injured animals receive the care they need.

On the public side, Riverside County Animal Services and the Moreno Valley Animal Shelter have developed a particular set of skills when it comes to managing wild burros and donkeys. They may very well be the two most knowledgeable government agencies when it comes to these creatures in the state. Just another secret skill set of the Inland Empire.

Rather than drive the canyons and encroach on private-property owners, find a "chance encounter" with a donkey while taking part in a Moreno Valley specific hike. A hike to the "M" is the safest bet for animal and human alike. From the lot to the hillside "M" is about two miles; the terrain is varied, but most would consider this an easy-to-moderate hike. Donkeys are regularly sighted at the parking lot and along the trail.

Water from Reche Canyon's mineral springs was believed to contain healing properties to cure all sorts of ailments. From the late 1800s to early 1900s, upwards of four hundred bottles a month were sold to customers around the country.

41 DO YOU HAVE THAT IN LEATHER?

Is this an early example of a "Made in Alta California" industry?

The Catholic Mission system established a trade route and several of the region's first permanent industries. In addition to vineyards, the other major agricultural holding they managed was cattle. These animals were valuable for their meat and their hides. The hides were the reason for the expansive trade routes established by European and US sailors, who braved treacherous weather around Cape Horn, at the southern tip of South America.

This commerce was perhaps first discussed at length in *Two Years Before the Mast*, an autobiography by Richard Henry Dana Jr., published in 1840. Besides becoming a seminal work on the life of a sailor, it captures the efforts of both sailor and Indian, in service to moving hides from the western coast of Alta California to the East Coast tanneries of the United States.

SERRANO TANNING VATS

WHAT First tannery established in the Inland Empire

WHERE 23730 Temescal Canyon Rd., Corona

COST Free

PRO TIP It's easy to miss as the area is used by big rigs for parking, just east of Interstate 15.

The introduction of cattle dramatically altered the region's economy, ecology, and living conditions.

These two vats were built in 1819 by the Luiseño Indians under the direction of Leandro Serrano, first non-Indian settler in what is now Riverside County. The vats were used in making leather from cow hides. In 1981 the vats were restored and placed here by the Billy Holcomb Chapter of E Clampus Vitus. Tanning vats converted an abundant local resource, cattle hides, into a raw material for the creation of leather goods, diversifying the local economy. Photos courtesy of Larry Burns.

The vats were an attempt to increase profits and make leather goods locally by establishing tanneries on the west coast. Better management of regional resources was the reason why Leandro Serrano, Californio rancher and the first non-Indian settler in Riverside County, worked with the Luiseño Indians to build two tanning vats. The finished products from this operation included shoes and clothing, various agricultural tools, and home furnishings. In a sense, the vats are evidence of the Inland Empire's first "shop local" campaign!

IT CAME FROM OUTER SPACE

What weighs over six thousand pounds and was discovered in the Old Woman Mountains of San Bernardino County? The second largest meteorite in the US, that's what!

Given the large footprint of the Inland Empire, there's no telling what may be hidden in its expansive deserts and mountain ranges. Each year of exploration and development reveals new discoveries. Prospectors happened on this iron meteorite in 1975. As the discovery occurred on land managed by the US Bureau of Land Management and was a find of national scientific interest, it became the property of the federal government.

Under the care of the Smithsonian Institution's Museum of Natural History, the meteorite was analyzed, verified, and then sent around the country on a museum roadshow. In 1980, the meteorite was returned to the Mojave Desert for permanent display.

But that's not the only rare find from the Mojave you can see here. This space doubles as an environmental educational center for area schools. The Desert Discovery Center's many interactive exhibits allow budding scientists to explore the flora and fauna unique to this area. The outdoor environment includes a garden, tortoises, and a pond full of Mohave Tui Chub.

This rare fish was believed to be extinct for decades, but it was rediscovered in the 1980s at the Desert Science Center at Zzyzx, about eighty miles to the north. Oases similar to the

The "cut" in the meteorite came courtesy of the Smithsonian Institution in Washington, DC, which studied and displayed this find in 1978.

This native plant and animal habitat is the ideal setting to interact with the popular desert tortoise without disturbing them in their natural environment. Carrying it out from its resting place in the Old Woman Mountains was impractical, but a copter borrowed from Marine Heavy Helicopter Squadron 363 easily plucked the three ton meteorite from obscurity. Photos courtesy of Larry Burns.

one simulated here can be found across the Mojave and Sonoran deserts, which make up the eastern half of the Inland Empire. But they often require considerable hiking to explore. This space, happily, lets you skip the heavy labor and get right to the enjoyment.

The pond is part of a breeding program to reintroduce the species to its native habitat in and around the Mojave River. The center also has a smaller tank indoors for an even closer look at this example of what is possible through scientific research and environmental stewardship.

THE DESERT DISCOVERY CENTER

WHAT Home of two rare local discoveries: the Old Woman Meteorite and the Mohave Tui Chub

WHERE 831 Barstow Rd., Barstow

COST Free; donations welcomed

PRO TIP Attend one of the center's weekly programs to get more hands-on exposure to the cultural resources of the California desert.

43 CIVILIZATION'S POWER SOURCE

What fueled the citrus boom here? Water—and electricity!

Welcome to the first hydroelectric plant built in North America. If asked to guess the location, people often pick a place farther east, often something picturesque such as Niagara Falls. But no, it was right here in the Inland Empire.

This eight-hundred-kilowatt plant, tiny by today's standards, was the first hydro facility in the world to commercially generate three-phase, alternating current (A/C) power. Why did that matter in the 1890s? Prior to this achievement, the only way to generate large amounts of electricity used direct current (D/C). The limitation of direct current is that it can, at most, travel five miles from its generation source. Imagine a world running on electricity that had to be generated every five miles, and you'll appreciate the impact this innovation had.

Electrical engineer Almarian Decker was brought in to overcome the many obstacles involved in this challenge. First, no motors at the time could handle this feat, so he literally had to invent new motors. Using experimental models of rotating

---

MILL CREEK HYDROELECTRIC PLANT #1

WHAT Historical marker and nineteenth century power station.

WHERE Head about a mile north of the Mill Creek Visitor center at 34701 Mill Creek Rd. The plant is the non-descript tan building that looks to be built in the middle of the river. The dirt path from the shoulder can be walked or driven (with care).

COST Free

PRO TIP On Garnet Street, visible from Highway 38, check out the folk art, including a towering twenty-foot Paul Bunyan, a rooster, and Lady Liberty.

The technological marvel housed here permitted electricity to travel long distances, paving the way for world-wide industrial development. Photo courtesy of Larry Burns.

magnetic fields developed by a more famous inventor, Nicola Tesla, Decker created a system so out of the box that Westinghouse refused to build them! New upstart power company, General Electric, agreed to give it a try.

That's another example of what's possible when there's a significant need and few people with the vision to carry it out. Because of this, Redlands had lots of ice, which kept the citrus fresh and cold for its long train ride.

Sadly, Decker died a month before the electricity started to flow. This location continued to fuel the Redlands citrus industry until 1934, when it was replaced by bigger and better equipment. Today, ninety percent of the power generated in the world is created by the methods that were first introduced right here in the Inland Empire.

This powerhouse is kept exactly as it looked when it was built in 1893.

CHILDREN'S ROOM AT CORONA PUBLIC LIBRARY (page 38)

SHIELDS DATE GARDEN (page 12)

A RETIREMENT COMMUNITY FOR HAPPY MEAL TOYS (page 8)

NOAH PURIFOY'S OUTDOOR DESERT ART MUSEUM (page 56)

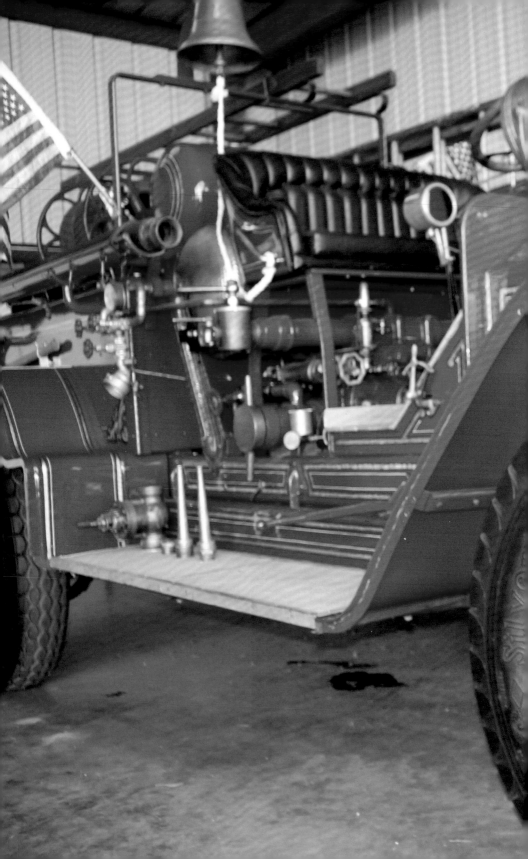

1925 ELSINORE FIRE TRUCK ENGINE #1 (page 132)

SKYPARK AT SANTA'S VILLAGE (page 150)

MALKI MUSEUM (page 166)

44 ADOBE HOMES FOR THE MODERN AMERICAN

What kind of dwelling works best in this climate?

Adobe construction—brought to North America from Central and South America via Mexico—was one of the earliest permanent housing structures of the American Southwest. This manner of construction mirrors the sensibilities of the Inland Empire: a dependence on local materials, simple construction, strong hands, and creative ideas that can handle the isolation and harsh climates of several regions. And with home construction one of the largest industries in the area as well, it's no surprise that a low-cost innovation based on traditional practices would take root in Hesperia.

Cal-Earth is a nonprofit that combines this traditional adobe building style with modern values and US building standards. They call it SuperAdobe. When founder Nader Kahlili sought a simple way to build safely while minimizing waste and environmental damage, his research led him to these traditional adobe structures. By modifying the methods and materials, he was able to achieve safety standards that exceeded those for traditional pitched-roof homes. And construction costs were reduced to a few thousand dollars.

CAL-EARTH

WHAT Education and manufacturing facility for adobe structures

WHERE 10177 Baldy Ln., Hesperia

COST Free group tours on the first Saturday of every month; $50 donation for private tours; various costs for workshops.

PRO TIP Grab the public tour and stick around for the potluck meal that's served afterwards to meet like-minded folks.

Nader Khalili, founder and inventor, envisioned a world constructed on the natural elements of earth, water, air, and fire, and their unity at the service of humanity. Why make domes? The arch is the strongest form in architecture and has been used in building for thousands of years. A dome is simply an arch rotated 180 degrees. Photos courtesy of Larry Burns.

The Cal-Earth grounds demonstrate the many creative ways the materials can be applied. These homes can be outfitted with just about any modern convenience you can name. How'd you like to be the first person on the block with a smart adobe? "Siri, load wood-burning fireplace!"

The designs created here exceed California's stringent earthquake standards.

45 WHERE ANIMATRONICS COMES TO LIFE

Who are the people behind those animatronic wonders?

Impact. It's one way to measure the influence of a region. Some of the biggest amusement-park destinations— Disneyland, Knott's Berry Farm, and Universal Studios among them—are known around the world. Lesser known, however, are the skilled craftspeople, artists, and entrepreneurs behind the animatronic wonders that people of all ages enjoy when they visit a theme park. Consider how boring the "Pirates of the Caribbean" ride at Disneyland would be without the contributions of the talented team that created the animatronic pirates carousing overhead.

The center of this universe is the Inland Empire, specifically, the labs of Garner Holt Productions, Inc. (GHP), where the innovative methods and memorable characters mostly originate. Hundreds of amusement parks, museums and training sites around the world feature GHP creations.

No single person has influenced the field more than Garner Holt himself. Growing up in San Bernardino, he found his calling when he was just eleven years old and created "Uncle Sam" as part of a 1976 "All American City" celebration. His Halloween haunted houses were the stuff of legend in the '70s and early '80s. Holt's creations have influenced generations and set the bar for what amusement-park entertainment should look like and be about.

Garner Holt Products, Inc. is the largest manufacturer of animatronics and animatronics figures in the world.

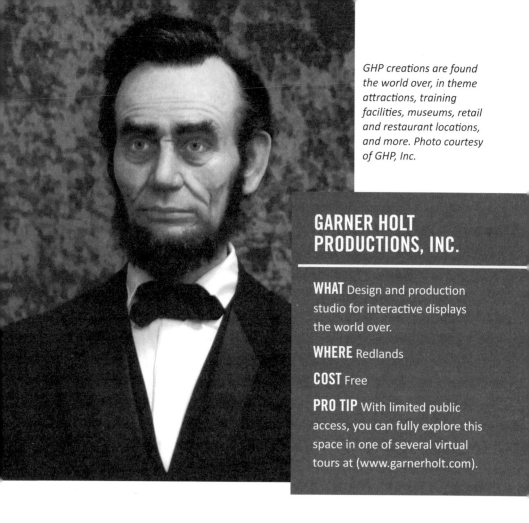

GHP creations are found the world over, in theme attractions, training facilities, museums, retail and restaurant locations, and more. Photo courtesy of GHP, Inc.

GARNER HOLT PRODUCTIONS, INC.

WHAT Design and production studio for interactive displays the world over.

WHERE Redlands

COST Free

PRO TIP With limited public access, you can fully explore this space in one of several virtual tours at (www.garnerholt.com).

But animatronics has gone far beyond entertaining technology. Today, it is used to train and educate in such diverse areas as health care and military defense.

In 2018, the headquarters moved from San Bernardino to provide more space for design and educational purposes. Why didn't the company move to a bigger metro? Simply put, it's the people. The geniuses who work alongside Holt also live in the area. There's something about the deserts and mountains and open spaces of the IE that attract talented creative types who simply refuse to leave! Fortunately, places like GHP will provide an outlet for all those creative expressions for decades to come.

46 DESERT MIRACLES

How did a fake sanatorium become a world-class research facility?

To create a sense of place takes generations working together in support of shared values. But if a person just wants to make a buck, well, that's much easier. Curtis Howe Springer was the type of charlatan who'd be drawn to the Inland Empire. Although he wasn't the first person to create a fake health spa, he may have been the hardest working and most creative.

A good deal of thinking went into his scam. First, he made up the name "Zzyzx" so the place name would always be the last on any list. Once his place was made up, he filed fake paperwork with the Bureau of Land Management, saying he was setting up a mining operation. His objective was to capture a small spring, called Soda Springs, and push it as a miracle cure and relaxation center.

For a while, the scheme worked—too well, actually. At times, water had to be trucked in to meet the demands for his miraculous "product." By the early 1970s, however, a long list of violations and misrepresentations closed the operation permanently.

Thanks to its remote location and limited commercial value, as well as the efforts of academics and civil servants, the place has thrived as an education center since 1976. For decades, it has worked to restore the natural oasis misused by its previous owner. Over time, the habitat has been restored, resulting in

The center's power is supplied by one of the world's largest photovoltaic substations. The ten-kilowatt substation was installed by Southern California Edison in 1995.

The center is situated at Soda Springs, a collection of groundwater seeps and springs along the western shore of Soda Dry Lake. Photo courtesy of Larry Burns.

the return of species currently threatened or even thought to be extinct.

Today, the site is no secret to biologists and California State University students. However, the facility's secret is that it is open to all guests with an educational interest. Management of the facility is by CSU Fullerton.

DESERT STUDIES CENTER

WHAT World-class environmental stewardship and conservation center

WHERE At the end of Zzyzx Road at Soda Springs (aka Zzyzx)

COST Free to visit; call 657-278-2428 for rental rates for day or overnight use of the facilities.

PRO TIP Ask about current research when you visit. The Mohave Tui Chub, thought extinct, was rediscovered here!

A TOO-COOL HOUSE

How did the IE stay cool before the invention of the A/C unit?

It's a fact: The Inland Empire delivers a pretty hot summer. This was simply another challenge faced by early communities of Native Americans. Solutions included the adoption of a nomadic lifestyle—echoed in modern times by the part-time residents of the IE, who spend the toastier months in another climate zone. The construction of adobes was another long-established way to keep indoor spaces cooler and avoid the harshest aspects of summer weather.

Think of the construction of the Rains house in 1860 as an early attempt at green building. Running beneath the original home was a diverted spring. Unfortunately, only sketches of that first-of-its-kind design remain. The cool water rushes below, pushing cool air into the home through the floor and open central plaza. Locally sourced red clay for the brick walls and a roof weatherized with tar from the La Brea Tar Pits keeps the most extreme weather at bay.

The relatively simple design uses the natural geography to full advantage. Breezes run consistently over the San Gabriel Mountains to the north. In warm weather, those result in the hot blasts of the sun known as the Santa Ana winds. But in the fall and early spring, those evening gusts make for refreshing times to enjoy the outdoors. This place makes your stay a breeze any time of the year.

JOHN RAINS HOME

WHAT Early ranchero home adapted to the local environment

WHERE 8810 Hemlock St., Rancho Cucamonga

COST $5 for adults; $4 for seniors/military; $2.50 for students; free for children under 5

PRO TIP The backyard features many artifacts typical of homes in this era, including a wagon. Hours: Tuesday–Saturday, 10 a.m.–3 p.m.

Little physical evidence remains of the climate control design beyond some drawings and oral accounts. It is believed that the first area school opened and was operated out of this home in 1870. Photos courtesy of Larry Burns.

JOHN & MERCED
RAINS' HOUSE
BUILT 1860-61

DATED BRICK
PLAQUE BY:
L.R. GORCZYCA
FAMILY

Unfortunately, John Rains, the original owner, didn't live long enough to enjoy many pleasant evenings. He was killed on the road while traveling to Los Angeles for business; his murder remains a mystery to this day. But in his lifetime, he was a lucky man. He married into one of the earliest land-owning Californio families. Working on John Williams' Chino ranchero, he was introduced to, and married Williams' older daughter, Maria Merced. Only days after the wedding, John Williams died unexpectedly, making Rains the part-owner of one of the largest rancheros in San Bernardino County—at least for a brief period.

Legends say that San Gabriel Mountain's Mount Baldy is domed because of the constant wind it experiences.

48 A FOUNTAIN OF YOUTH CONSTRUCTED OF SOUND WAVES

Did aliens from Venus really bring us the keys to immortality?

The Integratron bills itself as a blending of art, science, and magic. That description fits the deserts of the IE as well. Like a magician pulling flowered bouquets and live rabbits out of thin air, the desert, in its vibrancy, can surprise. Bursting quickly into life, it is rich with stories of those who thrive here.

Some believe the desert will show you things you need to see, when you're ready to see them. George Van Tassel spent a good part of his life looking and listening at Giant Rock (about three miles north of this site), and the Integratron was what he was told to create. His background as an aeronautical engineer and test pilot greatly informed the eventual creation of this dazzling white electronic machine.

Van Tassel was a staunch UFO advocate. He was one of several to organize events around UFO topics and attempts to make actual contact, a tradition that continues around here to this day. Unlike the rest, however, Van Tassel is the only one who claimed to have returned from a Venusian space ship with a formula to

INTEGRATRON

WHAT Sound baths delivered in an acoustically perfect structure

WHERE Corner of Belfield Boulevard and Linn Road, Landers

COST $35–$40 for public sound baths; $300 and up for private sessions (1-4 people).

PRO TIP Visit Giant Rock three miles to the north. Besides the inspiration point for Van Tassel, it is believed to be the world's largest free standing boulder.

The Integratron is built using a revolutionary design, all wood construction—sixteen glued and laminated spines held together like a Chinese puzzle by one ton of concrete at its apex. Photo courtesy of Larry Burns.

manufacture a sound frequency capable of restoring and repairing living tissue. His Giant Rock Spacecraft Conventions funded a nearly two decade construction process for his machine and drew thousands of devotees annually.

The finished product was not complete until the mid-1970s. Tragically, Van Tassel died unexpectedly two years later. Soon after his death, stories surfaced about missing secret notes and diagrams on related alien technology. Fortunately for mankind, the machine, and the mythology, live on to this day.

Consider sound as a nutrient for your nervous system. Quartz crystal singing bowls, keyed to the chakras of the body, provide peaceful relaxation and rejuvenation of mind and body.

49 A SECRET TRAINING CAMP FOR PEARL HARBOR RETALIATION

How has flight changed since the Wright Brother's historic lift-off at Kitty Hawk in 1903?

The growth of the Inland Empire was supported in large measure by the growth of US military might. One of the reasons that the Inland Empire remains diverse and broadly representative of the United States stems from this military history. Every branch of the service has a connection to this region. This particular location in Chino trained more than ten thousand pilots by the end of World War II. But it's the actions of some of its first trained pilots that made history.

Every school kid learns about the Pearl Harbor attack of December 7, 1941. Lesser known is the US retaliation in April 1942. Following months of planning and training, a bombing raid was successfully executed. A group of sixteen B-52s led by Lt. Col. Jimmy Doolittle boldly flew into the heart of Japan, striking the capital city of Tokyo. The bombs destroyed little of material value, but the message sent was clearly delivered. With no fuel for the return, most

PLANES OF FAME MUSEUM

WHAT Aviation history of America and the world

WHERE 14998 Cal Aero Dr., Chino

COST $15; reduced costs for veterans, seniors, and young children; free for active military and first responders. Hours: Weekdays, 10 a.m.–5 p.m.; Saturday, 9 a.m.–5 p.m.

PRO TIP Crave more aviation history? See the Fliers' Wall at the Historic Mission Inn Hotel and Spa, which includes a Lt. Col. Jimmy Doolittle recognition.

When the 75th anniversary of the raid was celebrated in 2017, there remained only one crewman still alive, 101-year-old Lt. Richard Cole, Doolittle's copilot. Photo courtesy of Larry Burns.

of the B-52s crash-landed in the sea. Amazingly, all but three crew members survived. Many went on to lead other campaigns and serve bravely in other dangerous missions to win the war in the Pacific.

Today, you can see examples of these planes and these fighters, placed alongside other notable aspects of aviation history. Several of the models here are the last of their kind and the only ones in the world still taking to the skies. Living artifacts such as the Northrop Flying Wing, the Boeing P-26 Peashooter, the Lockheed P-38J Lightning, and a Mitsubishi A6M5 Reisen (Zero) can be spotted around Chino on any given day. And you can spot them here, on the ground, for a small fee.

This museum is home to many "last-of-its-kind" airplanes, most of which are still flown regularly in the skies around this "flying museum."

A CANNON MORE OFTEN SEEN THAN HEARD

How did a two-hundred-year-old Mexican cannon wind up in San Bernardino?

This high-mileage cannon is the Forrest Gump of artillery. Meaning, it's been at the center of several interesting moments in California and Inland Empire history. Like many people who call the Inland Empire home, the cannon came from elsewhere. It first reached California in the early nineteenth century (when it was called "Alta California" and was part of Mexico) and helped Mexico keep pirates out of San Diego's harbor. Later, it saw work in the Battle of Cahuenga, defending the Californios during the Mexican-American War.

Independence Day, 1856 marks the cannon's introduction into IE history books. That year, patriotic San Bernardino held two parties: one for Mormons and another for independents (former Mormons and non-Mormons). The competition between the events was good-natured; people, food, and laughter crossed the lines throughout the day. At night, each camp rolled out a cannon and treated the gathering to dueling cannon fire.

In 1859, the cannon was part of an early dispute regarding slavery. Slavery was always illegal in California, and the state sided with the Union. However, two local physicians, A. Ainsworth and G.T. Gentry, future Unionist and Confederate

SAN BERNARDINO CANNON

WHAT A cannon used by two nations to resolve a handful of disputes

WHERE 2701 Del Rosa Ave. N, San Bernardino

COST Free

PRO TIP The marker for Fort Benson can be viewed at 601 S Hunts Ln. in nearby Colton.

Perhaps in recognition of its ability to find itself at the center of conflict, it's been encased in concrete, for everyone's safety! Photo courtesy of Larry Burns.

respectively, allowed their professional disagreements and personal animosity to spill from rhetoric to violence.

The pair first traded punches, then riding crops, and then bullets. When that didn't solve the issue, each side gathered friends, as well as more guns and booze. Amidst the revelry, someone remembered the cannon. Gentry's men surrounded Ainsworth's party, and prepared to end the disagreement with a close-range blast. Fortunately, a quick-witted Ainsworth supporter jammed the cannon, bringing an uneventful end to what became known as the Ainsworth–Gentry affair.

Today, the cannon sits peacefully outside the Native Sons of California building, waiting for either the next dispute or the next celebration. History tells us that the choice is ours.

The cannon played a "nonspeaking" role protecting the makeshift "Fort Benson" in the months prior to the Mormon Exodus of 1857.

51 TRAINING GROUNDS FOR THE US ARMY

Have you ever sat in an M-60 tank?

As the US Army seeks to preserve the stories of our country's conflicts in the twentieth and twenty-first centuries, part of its forward-looking mission is to develop exhibits that put a civilian in the boots of a service member. Those experiences, translated and interpreted in the George S. Patton Memorial Museum, are captured through an ongoing program that collects the personal histories of war veterans.

It's important to mention that the Inland Empire is home to the largest single interment location in the country for veterans, about a ninety-minute drive west of the museum at Riverside National Cemetery. Every day, more than thirty personal biographies are "lost." In this museum, those histories are not just stored, but restored and returned to a necessary place of prominence. The museum's hope is that you leave with a renewed sense of passion, pride, and patriotism.

Artifacts illustrate how weaponry has evolved over hundreds of years. Cannons demonstrate this perhaps most clearly. The museum has two reproductions of armaments designed by Leonardo da Vinci, whose advances improved distance, accuracy, reloading speed, and, most important, the safety of those using projectile weapons.

GEORGE S. PATTON MEMORIAL MUSEUM

WHAT Artifacts from World War I to Afghanistan

WHERE 62510 Chiriaco Rd., Chiriaco Summit

COST $8 for adults; $7 for seniors; $4.50 for children; free for veterans

PRO TIP If you want to explore the outdoor munitions during summer, show up before 11 a.m. or the heat will get you. Hours: 9:30 a.m. – 4:30 p.m., daily.

The Tank Pavilion features a Japanese Artillery Gun, as well as a M-60 turret. Have you ever wanted to sit inside a tank ? Well now you can! Established as the Desert Training Center, in WWII it trained over one million men. It was the world's largest military installation both in size and population stretching from Arizona to Nevada to California. Photos courtesy of Matt Burns.

As the tools of war continue to evolve, so too does the museum's collection. In 2017, the Matzner Tank Pavilion opened. If you've always wanted to sit inside a tank, for a thrill rather than by necessity, there's a beautifully restored M-60 tank you can climb in. Not for the claustrophobic, it provides a bit of the "feel" to go along with the biographies archived here.

During World War II, this land was part of the 18,000-square-mile Desert Training Center. Because of this, the area is popular with seekers of abandoned military hardware.

52 A SKIRMISH WITH FAMILY TIES

What's worth fighting for in the Inland Empire?

The rancho of Isaac Williams was the location of the Inland Empire's appearance in the Mexican–American War. At the time, Californios were the people of this area. They were the ranchers and educated class set up by the Spanish and the Catholic Church missions. Those two systems served to support one another in organizing land into agriculture and ranching, while pushing the native Indian population into missions or work on the ranchos.

Many of the fighters in this battle were related by blood or marriage, which may explain the small amount of actual blood shed on this battle site. One fatality was taken by the Mexicans, and three Americans were wounded. The battle was precipitated by concerns as to the loyalty of Isaac Williams, despite his marriage into José del Carmen Lugo's family and his taking of Mexican citizenship (required to own land in California under Mexico's authority). Not waiting to see which side Williams would take, a small band of troops moved in to prevent any surprise attacks.

BATTLE LINE OF THE MEXICAN–AMERICAN WAR

WHAT Former battle site, now a firefighter training facility

WHERE 4040 Eucalyptus Ave., Chino

COST Free

PRO TIP From 1858 to 1861, this site was also a stop for the famous Butterfield stage.

Hopefully, this is a footnote of America's last war with a neighbor.

SITE OF THE BATTLE OF CHINO
NEAR THIS SPOT ONCE STOOD THE HOME OF ISAAC WILLIAMS,
FIRST AMERICAN SETTLER IN THIS VALLEY, ABOUT WHICH ON
SEPTEMBER 26-27, 1846, WAS FOUGHT THE FIRST IMPORTANT
ENGAGEMENT IN CALIFORNIA OF THE WAR WITH MEXICO.
THIS WAS ALSO THE SITE OF THE CHINO RANCH STATION
OF THE BUTTERFIELD STAGE LINE, 1858-61.
ERECTED BY THE HISTORICAL SOCIETY OF
POMONA VALLEY, NATIVE SONS OF THE GOLDEN WEST
AND CIVIC ORGANIZATIONS OF CHINO VALLEY.
DEDICATED SEPTEMBER 28, 1946.

The little-known, inconspicuous State Historical Landmark No. 942, set in front of a fire station on Eucalyptus Avenue, commemorates the "Battle of Chino," the first victory by Mexican forces in the Mexican-American War. Californios defeat and captured 24 Americans, led by Benjamin D. Wilson, who were hiding in an adobe house in Rancho Santa Ana del Chino, near present day Chino, California. Photos courtesy of Larry Burns.

The siege on September 26 and 27, 1846, ended when the Mexicans threated to set fire to the roof of the ranch, forcing Williams and his contingent to surrender. The children were left in the safety of family members on the Mexican side, while the men were marched to Los Angeles and held several weeks. Due to the loss of Carlos Ballestreros during the brief gun battle, Lugo and others had to thwart attempts to hang the prisoners along the way. Once tempers had settled, the rebels were set free after a promise to refrain from causing any more trouble.

53 NOT THE STONE HOUSE OF THREE LITTLE PIGS FAME

How did this landmark survive a century of cultural and economic evolution?

The history of this region is replete with stories of artists relocating here to improve their health. Artist Ted Conibear had already established himself as a premier sand artist when he relocated to the IE for health reasons in the late 1950s. His health restored, he set about establishing a new arts studio, incorporating the Stone House into his one-hundred-acre biblical theme park that opened in 1957.

The house, an artifact from the area's history as a granite quarry, provided rest from the heat of the sun for the tireless laborers. Conibear applied a similar work ethic and passion, but on the much smaller medium of sand. His biblical representations captured key events from the New Testament, creating a buzz in the area. At its height in the 1960s, the theme park drew upwards of fifty thousand annually, due in no small part to its proximity to Highway 395.

By the early 1970s, the Temecula Valley was changing once again. The expansion of Interstate 15 gobbled up parts of 395 and BibleLand as well. Undeterred, Conibear reestablished the park in Yucaipa and continued to make new sculptures for his own pleasure and by commission until his death in 1994. A prolific artist, he made nine versions of da Vinci's *The Last Supper* alone.

The history of the historic Stone House began in the late 1800s during the time that the hills were being quarried for granite. The Stone House was used as a mess hall for the hard-working quarrymen. The workers were able to retreat from the sun to find comfort within its cool walls. Before Interstate 15 forced an exodus in 1971, a sculpture garden called Bible Land was tucked away between Rainbow and Temecula. More than 50,000 visitors a year wheeled into the 100-acre retreat. Photos courtesy of Larry Burns.

Where are those sculptures today? With many of the pieces crumbling away, the family elected to destroy the remaining works, leaving photos and memories. But the sculptures that Conibear created for private collections around the country may well live on, perhaps hidden in a backyard alcove or a roadside memorial.

Despite changes to industry, transportation, and recreation, the Stone House remains. You can see it on the ninth hole of Temecula Creek Inn's golf course. The house is open for weddings, special events, limited tours, or a peek while you search for your errant golf ball.

Surprisingly, Ted Conibear earned a good living and plenty of fame as a sand artist during the Great Depression.

A TOWN BUILT BY TV

From Hollywood's perspective, does the entire world look like a stage?

As noted on many pages of this book, the Inland Empire grew under the big shadow cast by the bright lights of Hollywood. The desert has provided recreation for A-level entertainers for as long as there has been an entertainment industry. What is more, the IE is a place of inspiration for countless movies. They are the stories of pioneers, cowboys, freed people, and dreamers who believed they needed nothing more than what a plot of land, a little water, and strong hands could create.

Explore the surrounding area to uncover lost secrets, or set out to make new discoveries. The nearby Pioneertown Mountain Preserve has places to match all hiking skill levels. Amateur sleuths can find evidence of old film sets and campsites that date back to well before the community was founded in 1946.

Producer Phil Krasne (*Cisco Kid* fame) and Roy Rogers are the men to thank for this place. They, as well as actors like Dick Curtis and Russell Hayden, were the visionaries behind this production and recreation center. The magic of this location is that the grounds could be used for shooting, as well as housing for the talent and the crew. Here, the streets are named to honor symbols of Hollywood cowboy spirit: Dale Evans, Annie Oakley, even the Red Ryder.

Today, Pioneertown is still an active stage for film production, but music lovers are the ones who are rushing into this town today. Pappy + Harriet's restaurant has legendary

---

The canyon road to this place from Yucca Valley is a California Scenic Route. Drive slowly.

Pioneertown Motel has stood since 1946 as a place for wearied travelers and sun-drunk revelers to seek solace and inspiration. Gene Autry played poker until sunrise in Room #9. Photo courtesy of Larry Burns.

PIONEERTOWN

WHAT 1880s Western town with (almost) all the modern amenities

WHERE 5040 Curtis Rd., Pioneertown

COST Free to walk the recreated main street attractions

PRO TIP Here are two phone numbers to help you get a head start on planning your visit: Pioneertown Motel, 760-365-7001; Pappy + Harriet's Food & Live Music, 760-365-5956.

waits for a table and legendary acts on its stage. Seriously, make a reservation—or plan to hang out an hour or two for a table (worth the wait).

The original Pioneertown Motel was fully restored in 2014 to harken back to the time when dozens of stars and crew would live here for weeks at a stretch. Each room is named after a guest who stayed there, and several have ghost stories and outrageous tales worthy of a *National Enquirer* cover story. You'll find dozens of historic photos and film artifacts to enjoy during your stay.

55 A GENERAL STORE SPECIFICALLY ABOUT THE 1930s

Could this be the internet of things, before the internet was a thing?

For those who say the pinnacle of twentieth-century confections was achieved before the invention of television, welcome to your Shangri-La. Wall to wall, floor to ceiling is the single best reproduction of a traditional general store from early-twentieth-century United States that you can find.

It is all too easy to get sucked into the retail aspect of the store. Lovingly reproduced over years of collecting and fine-tuning, the real treats here are the museum-quality artifacts. This is no reproduction. Each of the items is in its original packaging, and most even have their original ingredients inside! To add to the authenticity, the prices and the displays represent actual pricing and marketing practices during the 1930s.

In this era of Amazon's daily deliveries to your doorstep, it's easy to forget how hard finding basic necessities was for Western settlers. Many came to make their fortunes in mining and farming, but the real gold rush came to those who provided the raw materials to those dreamers. General stores supplied the laborers, and the families they supported, with standard frontier supplies: soap, food, cloth, toys, and games.

Jim Ruddy's remarkable collection represents decades of acquisitions and fortunate finds. Most items are the last of their kind—and irreplaceable.

It's hard to believe, but these all purpose general stores eventually morphed into the super retail centers found in every major city of America, and most of the developed world. Photo courtesy of Larry Burns.

General stores also served the growing needs of settled families, many without historical or familial ties to the area. Basic foodstuffs, clothing, and medicine were always in demand. For these families, the general store also served as a community center. In the era before texting and twenty-four-hour news, this was the place to meet up, share gossip, and talk about the weather.

RUDDY'S 1930s GENERAL STORE MUSEUM

WHAT Commercial goods experiencing a second life as museum pieces

WHERE 221 S Palm Canyon Dr., Palm Springs

COST $1

PRO TIP Try to discern which set of shelves in the store serves as a secret door into the offices of this compact museum!

WHERE YOU DO YOUR TIME FOR YOUR CRIME

How did they handle your right to a phone call?

Just outside the San Bernardino Historical and Pioneer Society sits a piece of history that's not often discussed but that's a simple fact of frontier life. What do you do with a bad guy when the law is in short supply? You lock the guy up until the law arrives. In some cases, it took a while for a judge to arrive from several towns over, so the holding cells had to be secure.

Peek inside this jail cell—the first jail in Southern California—and you'll notice that this small space has two bunks. I guess that explains why it's well ventilated.

Records are inexact, but most histories peg its first appearance in San Bernardino to the late 1850s. The increased need for a jail likely coincided with the growth in industry and an increased diversity of residents. Those competing desires and plans for the region sometimes resulted in conflict.

It was generally agreed that "something had to be done," but early reviews of the jail weren't positive. Some thought it was not sensible to hold people in this way, and others likened it to an animal cage, unsuitable for human habitation. Visit and decide for yourself. You may come away with a new appreciation for the Sixth Amendment of the US Constitution.

THE FIRST JAIL IN SOUTHERN CALIFORNIA

WHAT Early example of a holding cell for bad guys

WHERE Heritage House, 796 N "D" St., San Bernardino

COST Free outdoor display

PRO TIP Notice something strange at this corner? Its gradual angle was designed to accommodate wagon traffic. It's the last example found in San Bernardino.

Set in the outdoor patio, this artifact can be viewed outside normal museum hours. This jail cell was part of several private collections, including casino magnate Bill Harrah, before its donation to the San Bernardino Historical and Pioneer Society. Photos courtesy of Larry Burns.

This jail cell was constructed on the East Coast, sent "around the horn," and then made its way by wagon from San Francisco.

57 *REALLY* OLD SCHOOL FIRETRUCK

What's underneath that worn-out tarp?

Before 1972, Lake Elsinore was merely "Elsinore." But the lake has always been a part of this community's identity. In the late 1920s, Elsinore needed a fire engine to serve the growing town, and a machine was found that could draw water off the lake to battle a blaze. The 1925 American LaFrance Type-65 fire truck was part of regular fire service until the 1960s.

Is it a coincidence that the lake at Elsinore went dry for the first time in recorded history in the 1950s and stayed dry for ten years? Then, not long after it was refilled, the fire engine went missing for three decades. No dark conspiracies here. Like many things that once seemed indispensable, it was replaced by bigger and better equipment. Fortunately, rather than scrapped, it was forgotten until 1999.

Enter the Lake Elsinore Historical Society, which set about restoring this treasure from tires to its clapper bell. In a testament to the fire truck's fortitude, the tires were flat when they found the truck, but they held air! A full restoration with original equipment wasn't possible, however. It's believed that only three were made, and this one is the last of its kind. So, replacement parts, metal engine parts, and wooden inlays and spokes were handcrafted by volunteers.

Don't underestimate the power of elbow grease and a love of history.

Released for special events and parades, this one of a kind artifact spends most of its days "hanging out with the grandkids" at Station #10. Photo courtesy of Larry Burns.

1925 ELSINORE FIRE TRUCK ENGINE #1

WHAT How fires were fought in the Roaring Twenties

WHERE Winterfest Parade, corner of Library and Main Streets, Lake Elsinore

COST Free

PRO TIP Cover your ears when the fire truck goes by! One modern feature left off was the muffler.

The restoration team also made a few adaptations to modernity. First, the authentic—but uncomfortable—horsehair-stuffed cushions were replaced with foam. Second, they added a starter to replace the hand crank. Could you start an engine by hand crank?

Today, the only action that Lake Elsinore's first fire truck sees is in parades. You can catch a glimpse during city parades, such as Winterfest, which kicks off the first week of December annually.

What was considered "traveling in style" during the late 1800s?

The modern history of California is marked by the open road designed for the personal car. Regional historic roads such as Route 66 and Highways 38, 111, and 395 are special because their routes, and reroutes, shaped the community, saving some and consigning others to ghost towns and slowly decaying facades and billboards. The Gilman Ranch and Wagon Museum is one location where you can witness the evolution of travel in the western United States and learn how those changes affect a community.

The Victorian home that now serves as the museum is set within a large tract of land. During your visit, you can use the grounds for hiking, bird watching, or simply exploring the outdoor artifacts, which are given larger explanation in some of the indoor exhibits. For instance, you can walk a piece of the historic stage coach road and Bradshaw Trail. There's also an original adobe structure, the

GILMAN RANCH AND WAGON MUSEUM

WHAT Artifacts and records on transportation history and frontier living

WHERE 1901 W Wilson St., Banning

COST $4 for adults; $3 for kids; $1 for dogs.

PRO TIP Be aware that this museum has very limited hours: 10 a.m.– 4 p.m. on the second and fourth Saturday of every month.

This site's evolution from transportation hub to cattle ranch to fruit orchard to historical museum shows how living conditions changed over the last two centuries.

Once just an adobe hut, then a stage stop and general store and finally an expansive ranch house, the Gilman Ranch site remains today a storybook of the past. Surrounded by cottonwoods and watered by three natural springs, the present Gilman Ranch site has attracted people throughout time. The superb location of this canyon with an exceptional food and water supply offered a prime habitation site for the Cahuilla Indians in this area. Top photo courtesy of Pat Murkland, bottom photo courtesy of Larry Burns.

first permanent structure built on this site in 1854. In 1909, this was the site of the infamous "Willie Boy" murder and manhunt.

Inside, you'll find the most complete collection of nineteenth-century wagons, buggies, and stagecoaches in Southern California. The related journals and domestic tools, combined with the restored buildings that make up this property, provide a real sense of life on the frontier in the days before indoor plumbing, consistent law enforcement, and disease-fighting medications.

59 HOW FOG MADE SAN JACINTO FAMOUS IN MOSCOW

The Russians have landed! Hooray?

It's an understatement to say the United States and Russia have a complicated history. We've been close allies and bitter enemies.

PLAQUE MARKING RECORD-SETTING AVIATION ACHIEVEMENT

WHAT First successful transpolar flight, celebrated by frenemies the US and Russia

WHERE 2450 Cottonwood Ave., San Jacinto

COST Free

PRO TIP The memorial is adjacent to Fire Station #78. The actual landing site is about three miles west. Due to vandalism, the memorial was moved to this more visible location in 2006.

This heartwarming story starts in Moscow and ends with a ticker-tape parade for Russian pilots in our nation's capital. It's an exciting aviation tale that put one of Riverside County's oldest cities on the map—again!

It was 1937, and flying machines were still a novelty experienced mostly by the wealthy or members of the armed services. Each year, it seemed a new aviation record was made or shattered. In the 1930s, the successful culmination of a nonstop transpolar flight (that's the kind that goes over the North Pole or the South Pole) was a bit of a Russian obsession.

The ANT-25 that completed the mission, which was perfect for long, record-shattering flights but little else, was decommissioned soon afterward.

The flight crew consisted of Mikhail Gromov (pilot), Andrei Yumashev (co-pilot), and Sergei Danilin (navigator). The aviators were taken to March Air Base (now March Air Reserve Base), in Riverside, for rest and recuperation. The Tupolev ANT-25 was a Soviet long-range experimental aircraft. First constructed in 1933, it was used by the Soviet Union for a number of record-breaking flights. Photos courtesy of Larry Burns.

In this case, Santa's northern outpost was buzzed by not one, but two attempts to make the record. Both originated in Moscow. The first, on June 17–20, came up short of its San Francisco destination and made an emergency landing in Vancouver, WA. The second effort, July 12–14, finally made it to California but again missed the expected destination: Lindbergh Field in San Diego (now known as San Diego International Airport).

The failure of the second attempt, however, was not due to mechanical problems. The cause was natural: the weather—fog, to be exact. With everything between San Diego and Los Angeles shrouded, the pilot navigated east a bit, then a bit more, until the aircraft was one hundred miles from the destination and very low on fuel. The three-man crew found a flat-enough cow pasture and safely landed in San Jacinto, covering 7,120 miles in sixty-two hours.

The crew members were welcomed as heroes, with a parade and a visit with President Franklin Roosevelt at the White House. Folks came for months to see the incredible hulking silver miracle that had fallen from the sky. The plane is no more. Oddly enough, it was disassembled and shipped back to Russia by freighter! But the plaque remains, a testament to the reach of mankind, with a little help from the bovines.

137

WALK THE SPANISH TRAILS

What can you learn by visiting an old cemetery?

The Old Spanish Trails served as a vital commerce corridor that cut through the southwestern United States, from Los Angeles to New Mexico. What stitched the two ends together were fledging outposts to support commerce and replenish supplies. Between 1842 and 1845, two communities established themselves on land owned by Juan Bandini and Antonio Lugo. Californio settlers came up from Mexico, led by patriarch Lorenzo Trujillo. Trujillo and his sons established "La Placita de los Trujillos" (later shortened to La Placita) on the eastern side of the Santa Ana River. A few years later, they established a second town, Agua Mansa, on the river's western shore.

Ranches expanded, commerce increased, and at its peak in the 1860s, the region was second only to Los Angeles in size. As in many towns, the chapel and the cantina were the centers of activity.

The cantina, however, was no ordinary watering hole. A desire to limit the political power of this large community of Californios made the bar infamous overnight. As American and European immigration increased, officials made sure the new boundary between Riverside and San Bernardino Counties bisected this prosperous Latino community.

AGUA MANSA PIONEER CEMETERY

WHAT Insights into the past at California State Historic Landmark #121

WHERE 2001 East Agua Mansa Rd., San Bernardino County

COST $5 for adults; $4 for seniors/military; $2.50 for students/children; free for kids under 5

PRO TIP The original chapel bell is "hidden" in the gardens of the Mission Inn Hotel and Spa in Riverside. Hours: Tuesday–Saturday, 10 a.m.–3 p.m.

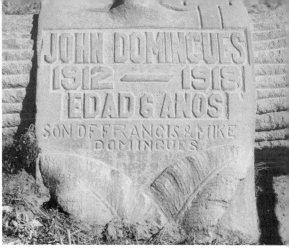

In the 1840s, this was the largest settlement between New Mexico and Los Angeles. Today, the Agua Mansa Pioneer Cemetery is nearly all that remains of these once-thriving communities. The Trujillo cantina closed in World War II, and the last burial in the cemetery occurred in 1963. Photos courtesy of Larry Burns.

The new political boundary ran right down the cantina's dance floor. Back then, San Bernardino was a dry county, no alcohol; Riverside wasn't. When police came to raid the "speakeasy," patrons lifted their glasses and calmly walked with them to the Riverside County side of the bar. The police left with their paddy wagons empty.

The cemetery and the nearby Trujillo Adobe are the last major artifacts of this period. A sign of the times, both have been encroached on over the decades. They now stand in isolation, surrounded by an industrial corridor of roads, railways, and warehouses carrying consumer goods to all corners of the country.

The cemetery is fortunate to have a full-time caretaker, but the last burial on this site took place in 1963. After you walk the grounds and appreciate the artisans responsible for the headstones, you can learn more about the prominent citizens buried here by viewing the additional documents and artifacts housed in the adjacent museum.

The site was formally made part of the Old Spanish Trails in 2017.

61 A YELLOW BEACON FOR YOUR FUEL UP

What did service stations look like one hundred years ago?

Fully restored by determined volunteers in 2015, at the centennial anniversary of this historic site, this service station is a snapshot into the not so very long ago. Although experiencing lots of love today, this place, as well as many parts of Historic Route 66, have been lacking in love for some time.

Service stations such as these popped up quickly in the early part of the twentieth century, meeting the growing car craze in America fueled by Ford's Model T a decade earlier. This is a Richfield service station, complete with a large collection of Richfield-branded artifacts and creations. What has been restored here provides a sense of what people needed on the road.

Roads shaped the history of the Inland Empire. Across this area, roads brought civilization. Starting with the early hunting paths and migration patterns of nomadic tribes, travel across the vast spaces of the Inland Empire was no easy task. New modes of transport increased the number of travelers and settlers, while making the journey less dangerous.

But there were still negative effects. The stagecoach increased the speed of travel and established new towns but destroyed previous trade routes. Later, the train usurped the

This restored location is a stunning example of gas station architecture from early twentieth-century America.

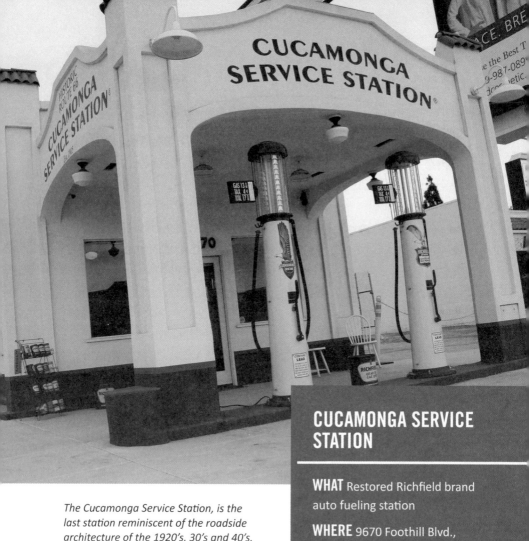

The Cucamonga Service Station, is the last station reminiscent of the roadside architecture of the 1920's, 30's and 40's. Photo courtesy of Larry Burns.

CUCAMONGA SERVICE STATION

WHAT Restored Richfield brand auto fueling station

WHERE 9670 Foothill Blvd., Rancho Cucamonga

COST Free

PRO TIP Why is this restored service station bright yellow? The restoration team uncovered the original paint job under a boring white coat, then color-matched it. Hours: Thursday–Sunday, 10 a.m.–3 p.m.

wagon, leaving countless rutted roads to return to their natural state. Next came automobiles, eighteen-wheelers, and an interstate super-highway system. Today, in our new virtual world, those old systems are threatened by massive transit hubs and the growing allure of never leaving our homes.

62 HEAVEN FOR CAR LOVERS

How did the automobile affect daily life?

The Motte family were early pioneers who settled in the Perris Valley and established several successful agricultural operations that grew and expanded under successive generations. The barn was created to sell the fruits and veggies of those operations in 1985. Each piece of wood and metal in the barn was salvaged from other structures in the area. So when you walk through the modernized barn door, you'll see local history reused at every turn.

This museum exists because the family wanted to preserve early pioneer history. They did so by curating the tools used in agriculture, as well as some of the machines used to cultivate and harvest crops of all kinds. You'll also be treated to some nostalgia-inducing recreations: an olde tyme theater for moving pictures and a soda fountain tableau straight from the nifty fifties.

MOTTE HISTORICAL MUSEUM

WHAT Complete car collection covering the early to mid-1900s

WHERE 28380 Highway 74 E, Menifee

COST Free

PRO TIP Don't miss the second floor, with artifacts of early Perris Valley history, including Perris's first jail cell. Hours: Wednesday–Sunday, 10 a.m.–4 p.m.

Steve McQueen was integral to the racing scene of the IE. A photo on the wall captures him as he signs a check to purchase another item for his collection.

Leon E. Motte built the Motte's Romola Farms Barn in 1985 with architect Robert Morris. Robert Morris has done much architectural design in downtown Temecula, and is known for his wrought iron work and western artistic touch. The cars illustrate the importance of the combustion engine in transportation, recreation, and agriculture. Photos courtesy of Larry Burns.

But the cars are the main attraction. The vehicles here span the essentials of a bustling town: police cars, school buses, firetrucks. Painstakingly restored, these are early- to mid-twentieth-century restorations of vehicles actually in use around Perris Valley in their day. They appear to need little more than the turn of a key—or in some cases, several turns of the crank—to be ready for their next tour of Inland Empire hot spots.

63 ANOTHER ROADSIDE ATTRACTION

Can you point me towards 1950?

Amboy was a popular place to stop, refill the gas tank, and feed the family as people travelled and explored across the state and the Southwest. But the Amboy of today is a shadow of that former roadside attraction. Over the years, the buildings have come, then gone to decay. The people came, then they left.

A few people saw potential in the faded signs and dusty corners of this place. When it came up for sale—it was listed on eBay, naturally—restaurateur Albert Okura (aka, "The Chicken Man") snatched it up, hoping to preserve this unique treasure. He restored several buildings, including the post office, the café, and the gas station.

According to "The Chicken Man," many gas stations along Route 66 began to falter by the late 1990s. Those that survived had to modernize their tanks and related equipment; environmental stewardship standards were upgraded a bit since the 1950s. This station—likely the only gas station left with the original pumps dating to the original Route 66—is now outfitted with recent technology. Lovingly restored, this gas station is the kind seen in black-and-white movies, featuring white-coated technicians hard at work to speedily service cars and get them back on the road.

As you fill your tank—by yourself—listen as the rolling dials make a pleasant clickity-clack. And while you wait, you can gaze on an even more famous and durable feature: the Amboy crater. It was here long before all of this, and it will certainly be here long after the last remnants of Route 66 return to the sands from which they sprang.

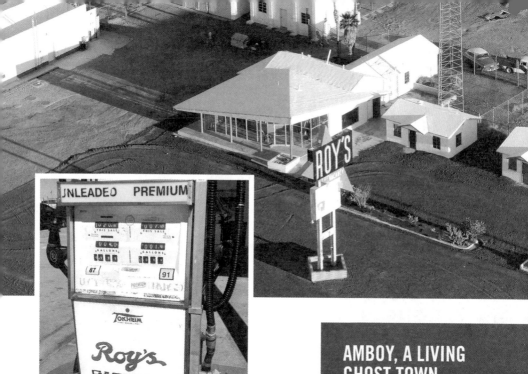

The historic site is an example of roadside Mid-Century Modern Googie, characterized by space age designs symbolic of motion, such as boomerangs, flying saucers, diagrammatic atoms and parabolas. Albert Okura, the current owner of the city of Amboy and it's structures, is committed to preserving the town in much the way it appeared during its Route 66 heyday. Photos courtesy of Manny Lopez.

Albert Okura, aka "The Chicken Man" and founder of Juan Pollo restaurants, bought this town for just under $500K in the early 2000s.

64 SPORTS FOR THE REST OF US

What has four legs, three balls, and flippers?

If you collect ten old arcade machines and cram them into your duplex's garage, you're an eccentric guilty of violating many zoning codes. But if you collect more than one thousand, outfit an airplane hangar for the lot of them, and open your doors to the public, then that makes you a visionary.

The team that keeps these machines running in optimal shape deserves a museum of their own. It is no easy task keeping over a thousand machines in top working condition.

Since 2013, professional 'ballers and the casual fan pay homage to the arcade gods two or three times a year when this place is open to the public. Those long weekend events feature around-the-clock free play, as well as tournaments with purses that can run over a thousand bucks.

When you're here—and advance planning is critical—a single admission fee provides you the keys to the castle. One side of the facility houses all the pinball machines. On your first visit,

MUSEUM OF PINBALL

WHAT Hundreds of fully restored arcade games

WHERE 700 S Hathaway St., Banning

COST $40 for a day pass; $95 for a three-day pass

PRO TIP Only open 2-3 times per year for special events and tournaments. Check website (www.museumofpinball.org). Events need volunteers, sign up and save on your admission and tournament play.

Classic arcades provide low-cost daycare for Generation X.

More than just a museum, the grounds play host to several sanctioned pinball tournaments each year, and is a must see destination for any ranked professional. Photo courtesy of Larry Burns.

play that favorite machine of yours right away. Get it out of your system, relive those cherished memories, and then find some new ones. The layout changes, but there's an organizational structure here. Most machines are organized by decade and then by brand.

The other side of the facility is for all the other arcade games you know and love—plus a few hundred you've probably never heard of. In addition to the stand-alone classic arcades, you'll find working models of most of the at-home video game systems that changed entertainment in the 1980s and then became indispensable to households by the 2000s.

Is this the pinball hall of fame? Many ask this question, but the official Pinball Hall of Fame is about 270 miles away in Las Vegas. In January 2015, the Museum of Pinball earned a spot in the *Guinness Book of World Records* for hosting the largest number (311) of simultaneous pinball players.

65 COME FOR THE MINERAL SPRINGS, STAY FOR A COUPLE OF YEARS

How did a four-star resort become government surplus?

The Norconian's origins, rise, and long fall mirror the hopes and dreams of the nation, this community, and the long-term pursuit of the American Dream. The visionary behind its inception was Rex Clark, whose name seems to fit the go-go era of pleasure and profit that epitomized the 1920s. But his first strike at fortune didn't go as planned. While drilling for oil in alfalfa fields, he hit a hot mineral spring. Ever the entrepreneur, he expanded his vision and created a private compound of outdoor recreation, original entertainment, and legendary parties. This stunning-in-its-time example of new mission revival architecture drew the rich, powerful, and famous from the confines of Los Angeles. Here, they could unwind and relax from the rigors of running the world.

A victim of possibly the worst imaginable timing, the hotel opened in February 1929. The world-class equestrian trails, pools, gardens, sports facilities, and envious amenities—this place had its own private airport—were the talk of the town until its final curtain call as an entertainment destination in 1941. The Navy purchased the site a few months before the Pearl Harbor attack and converted the hotel into a hospital. Its first patients were survivors of that attack.

NORCONIAN

WHAT Former playground of Hollywood elite

WHERE 1999 Fourth St., Norco

COST Free

PRO TIP The former hotel—still a stunning example of Mission Revival Style architecture—is visible from the western side of nearby Norco College.

On February 2, 1929, The Norconian Resort was given to the world with a star-studded grand opening. Complete with boating, an airfield, horseback riding, mineral-baths, tennis, golf and swimming; the resort attracted celebrities, Olympians and even some politicians. Photo courtesy of Kevin Bash. In September–October 1941, the United States Navy purchased the resort, and on December 8, 1941, the day after Pearl Harbor, the resort was commissioned the United States Naval Hospital in Corona. Photo courtesy of Larry Burns.

The Navy's taking up this well-appointed resort may be surprising, but even more incredible is the other neighbor to take up residence: a women's prison! Given these strange bedfellows, the location is difficult to access. Currently, the site is isolated and boarded up, unused. Sadly, what started as a beacon of hopes and dreams in the twentieth century is today a slowly decaying artifact of the Inland Empire. Efforts continue to save and restore this historic building.

On March 18, 1947, two paraplegic teams— Norco's Rolling Devils and a team from Birmingham Veteran's Hospital—played the world's first organized game of wheelchair basketball.

66

THE REAL NORTH POLE

This staycation brings the North Pole to Southern California.

This park was the first franchised amusement park built in the United States, arriving on the entertainment scene months ahead of Disneyland. For many years, attendance here handily beat the gate at the home of Mickey Mouse. And what's not to love? Families could interact with animals, including live reindeer, in the petting zoo; and carnival rides, live shows, and chances to get a good word in with St. Nick months before the holiday rush kept families coming back year after year.

By the late 1980s, however, the fun spot found itself competing with much bigger, more centrally located attractions. By 1998, this North Pole turned off its reindeer runway.

But the park stayed alive in many people's hearts and minds—especially Michelle and Bill Johnson's. Bill had his first job in the original Santa's Village, so buying and restoring the property was a bit of a homecoming. In December 2016, the new, improved park was ready to reassume its place in the Inland Empire entertainment spotlight.

Gone are the zoo animals and garish carnival rides. Today, the modernized park focuses its recreation on using the naturally beautiful environment. Outdoor recreation on the miles of mountain-bike trails—hiking and rock climbing, and specimen

Following 2003's "Old Fire," Skypark's meadow became a staging area to remove tens of thousands of dead trees from the forest. After a multi-year habitat restoration, the Wetland Preserve is functioning once again—and worth a visit in the spring for the fanciful blooms.

This is where Santa lives year-round! Experience the wonder of nature as you enjoy biking, hiking, fishing, archery, ziplining and climbing in the Northwoods. Photo courtesy of SkyPark at Santa's Village.

collection and observation—draws visitors from around the state and the world. There's even a "mineshaft" for kids to experience the life of a nineteenth-century prospector.

Santa's House and the Gingerbread House Bakery are places that must be explored—and their wares tasted! Children can take part in several arts-and-crafts projects, participate in storytelling, and even spend some quality tea time with Mrs. Claus. The monorail is still in place, and the historic bumble bee cars that are iconic to the village are displayed around the park.

During bankruptcy, many of the artifacts of the first village were purchased by local residents. So keep your eyes peeled for the examples of the red mushrooms, and related statuary, installed on the front yards of several area homes.

SKYPARK AT SANTA'S VILLAGE

WHAT One of California's earliest amusement parks, renovated and ready for fun

WHERE 28950 State Hwy. 18, Skyforest

COST $10 for parking; $24–$39 for entry (free for children under three and seniors)

PRO TIP Open days (and prices) change by season, so be sure to call ahead to 909-744-9373.

67

SEE IT LIKE IT WAS SHOT

Where can you still watch 16mm and 35mm films for free every week?

Casual film fans focus on star power and story, but aficionados of the craft pay attention to how films are made and presented. Focusing there brings together elements of history, technology, and storytelling in a way that makes clear how movies have dazzled audiences for over a century.

The purpose of watching film this way is to replicate, as much as possible, the original filmmaking experience. So if a movie was shot on 35mm film, the best way to duplicate the experience and vision of the filmmaker is to view it in the same format.

With both 16mm and 35mm projectors at the ready, you can expect a "new" classic film every Monday. The rules are simple: no phones and no talking. Seating is no frills, and you bring your own snacks. This pared-down experience closes each week with a discussion among viewers. Sometimes, a guest speaker will introduce a film and share interesting pieces of film trivia you won't find on an

FREE FILM SCREENINGS AT REDLANDS VINYL RECORDS

WHAT Classic films featuring engaging conversation in a novel setting

WHERE 214 E Redlands Blvd., #200, Redlands

COST Free

PRO TIP Films start at 7 p.m., and late arrivals are frowned on.

Combining his years of running theaters with his love of vinyl records, proprietor Dave Bernal created a wicked cool blend of analog nostalgia and celluloid entertainment.

There's a little bit of everything under this roof. The not for sale items include gold records and posters from the world renowned Swing Auditorium of San Bernardino. Film and music are forms of entertainment that can stand on their own, but are made even greater when combined by a talented group of artists. Photos courtesy of Larry Burns.

IMDb listing. Occasionally, the screenings include a comedy lineup as well. On those nights, donations are appreciated to cover the cost of the professional talent.

By day, the place disguises itself as a vinyl record shop with many rare pressings and collectable posters. In terms of regional history, it has some of the only remaining artifacts from Swing Auditorium, which was destroyed by a plane crash in the 1980s.

There's a sister location in Palm Springs at 220 N Palm Canyon Drive. There, weekly outdoor screenings are hosted on the patio of Gré Coffee House and Art Gallery. This is easily the best spot to appreciate all the ways film and music connect back to the people and places of the IE.

68

FADE TO BLACK

Didn't we almost have it all?

Pomona was made famous in no small measure by detective-story writer Raymond Chandler and his gritty protagonist, Phillip Marlowe. This was the location of the orange groves that the goons from Los Angeles would drive to in order to bury their problems. Perhaps his inspiration for those apocryphal tales came from the real-life story of Spadra's founder, Arkansas native William "Uncle Billy" Rubottom.

Two significant pieces of history mark the Spadra Cemetery. It was the first non-Catholic cemetery in the area. More importantly, it was across the street from Uncle Billy's bar. Now, guns were banned from the bar, but Uncle Billy was OK with knives. Legends say that when a bar fight turned deadly, the evidence could be dragged across the street for a quick moonlit ceremony. While farfetched, many actual murder mysteries connect back to the infamous bar. Those, in turn, fueled plenty of ghost tales, which became even more plentiful following the "death" of Spadra.

In reality, Spadra didn't die. But dependent on the stagecoaches, the community suffered when the railroad line was extended and the depot located in Colton.

The town may have failed, but the cemetery is experiencing life anew—and not just the ghostly variety. The Historical

SPADRA CEMETERY

WHAT Lasting remnant of a boom-and-bust town

WHERE 2850 Pomona Blvd., Pomona

COST $20 for the tour

PRO TIP Private tours can be scheduled. Contact the Historical Society of Pomona Valley (909-623-2198) for fees and arrangements.

Is it ironic that a "town that died" has been kept alive by the preservation of its cemetery? There are many possible sources, but no one can say for certain who put this expensive memorial marker in place. Photos courtesy of Larry Burns.

"THE END OF THE TRAIL"
URSULA PONEDEL MEYER
JUNE 16, 1903 — SEPT 29 1935

Society of Pomona Valley, with help from students at nearby CSU Pomona, takes care of the 205 souls buried behind its gate, which is closed 364 days a year. A special docent-led tour is scheduled annually on All Hallows Eve, from 7 p.m. until midnight. Get your scares, hear a bit of fun local history, and "meet" some of the first American settlers of the Pomona Valley at Spadra Cemetery.

One of the Inland Empire's first cities, Spadra was eclipsed and later incorporated by Pomona in the 1950s. Boom to bust in less than a century.

69

BODHISATTVA QUAN YIN RISES ALONG HIGHWAY 395

Why not cultivate mindfulness in a tranquil high desert oasis?

On the list of reasons why people came to this part of California, health is definitely in the top five. The Mojave and Sonoran deserts that run across a good portion of the Inland Empire were seen as pristine, albeit sparse, places to repair one's health. The use of the health spas and healing hot springs here often predates European exploration and US expansion.

In view of this history, the appearance of several dozen austere white Buddhas along Highway 395 in Adelanto seems like just another example of healing taking place in the Inland Empire. This working Vietnamese Buddhist temple supports parishioners from around Southern California.

With the exception of special ceremonies, the place is open every day of the year from dawn until dusk. The exterior grounds and the interior are worth close study and enjoyment. Start at the far end of the pavilion, and enjoy dozens of elaborately carved representations of Buddha and Buddhist ideals.

Those with more experience with western religions than eastern traditions will find the "stained glass" stories running along the walls to be informative. They illustrate the values and history shared in various Sutras that serve as the

The location serves practitioners hailing from all corners of Southern California.

Bodhisattvas venerated here, in particular Quan yin, are sought out for their spiritual guidance and sometimes, powerful worldly assistance in such mundane areas as job seeking and finding love. Photo courtesy of Larry Burns.

inspiration behind the images you'll see and the prayers you'll hear during your visit.

Many incredible tales are told about the Healing Buddha at the center, Bodhisattva Quan Yin. Her visage comes to several parishioners, often while traveling to or from the center. And she's been known to provide a miracle or two in order to convince doubters. More than one person has captured well-timed cell-phone shots in which the statue seems to disappear before one's eyes. A contrast between white clouds and the white statue could be the reason, or something more existential could be at play. You decide which.

157

70

FAMILY-FRIENDLY OFF-ROAD RACING

Who was Harvey Mushman?

What do you do when racing is in your blood, but the people who own your blood don't want you to race? You cheat the system by changing your name! At least that is all it took for Steve McQueen. In the 1960s, the same decade that Elsinore inaugurated the Elsinore Grand Prix, the all-access race drew big names, including local racing legend Malcolm Smith and Hollywood star Steve McQueen. Most raced just for fun. McQueen, obligated by his studio contract to avoid "extracurricular risky activities," used the pseudonym "Harvey Mushman" when he raced. The "Harvey Mushman 100" is named in McQueen's honor, even though Smith won the race handily most years.

(LAKE) ELSINORE GRAND PRIX

WHAT Annual multiday street race held in early November that turned fifty in 2018

WHERE Lake Elsinore Diamond Stadium at Main St., Lake Elsinore

COST Free

PRO TIP Unless you're competing, extreme enjoyment can be yours by partaking of the dozens of activities along Main Street.

One would expect that national coverage of a small dirt-bike race would be a welcome development. But the documentary *On Any Sunday*, from Bruce Brown, only served to draw huge, rowdy crowds and drive away the celebrities. So by the mid-1970s, the races were shut down permanently.

Like many great things from the 1960s and 1970s, the Lake Elsinore Grand Prix made a spectacular comeback in the 1990s. Now focused on serving the family-friendly racing crowd,

GRIPSTERS M.C.
Presents

ELSINORE
100 MILE
GRAND PRIX

★ RIDE A TRUE GRAND PRIX ★

9 mile course through the town and surrounding countryside of picturesque Elsinore, Calif.

City Streets —— Highways —— Byways

FEB. 10 & 11 Rain or Shine

BIG BIKES SUN. AMA SANCTIONED SMALL BORES SAT.

DISTRICT 37 POINTS SCRAMBLES AND DESERT

Mail entry only
Entry fee - $10

No refunds

Entries now open
Close Jan. 27 midnight

Mail to:

ABC
Wide World of Sports
will be there

Start position
determined by postmark

We assign numbers

King size trophies
MUCHO FUN

The Elsinore Grand Prix is a dirt-bike race that takes place in and around the Lake Elsinore area. Closed down by "too much fame" and unruly crowds, it is now a day long series of family friendly racing events designed to showcase local cultural history and good-hearted competition. Photos courtesy of Steve Miller.

it still holds races on a mixture of traditional tracks and downtown streets. The races are still open access, inviting anyone who feels up to the challenge to step right up. And, of course, the "Harvey Mushman 100" is a signature event. It's one of several dozen competitions, testing the skills of amateurs and pros alike, in an urban setting that retains plenty of examples of its historical features.

The 1971 documentary *On Any Sunday*, by legendary documentarian Bruce Brown, captured the early history of these races.

71

A GIFT OF FRIENDSHIP FOR THE WORLD

What would you do to bring an end to war?

To reach this location, you have to ascend Mount Rubidoux, a summit featuring a white, thirty-foot cross that's iconic and rich with history. Lesser known, but equally reflective of the values and the vision of many civic leaders, is the Peace Tower and Friendship Bridge. Besides the history, this spot provides a bird's-eye view of Fairmount Park. (Note for students of architecture: The Olmsted brothers, sons of Central Park architect Fredrick Law Olmsted, designed Fairmount Park.) Over six thousand people walk, jog, and bike past the Peace Tower and Friendship Bridge every month and likely have no clue what it represents. For them, and you, here's the scoop.

Built in 1925, the tower and bridge were dedicated to Frank Miller by his friends, who wanted to commemorate the man's lifelong pursuit of friendship and world peace. The dedication in December of that year coincided with a long period of travel around the Orient by Frank Miller and his sister, Alice Richardson.

Earlier, in 1911, Miller had established a peace conference in concert with the Andrew Carnegie Peace Foundation. Like many others in the period immediately prior to World War I, Miller saw a world on the brink of war and believed that recognizing the inherent value of all the countries of the world was the recipe for world survival. Then, in 1919, in furtherance of his goal of worldwide peace, Miller established an Armistice Day sunset

---

Frank Miller, best known as the first innkeeper of the Mission Inn Hotel and Spa, co-founded the Institute of World Affairs to address world peace.

The site of this feature, Mt Rubidoux, never panned out as a financial success. But it's cultural impact can be measured by the 6000 or more people who walk beneath this bridge each month. Photo courtesy of Larry Burns.

PEACE TOWER AND FRIENDSHIP BRIDGE

WHAT A gift of friendship for the world along the path of Mount Rubidoux

WHERE Mount Rubidoux summit; park at 5000 Tequesquite Ave., Riverside

COST Free

PRO TIP Stand at the cross to capture a vivid picture of the Peace Tower and Friendship Bridge with the American flag. The flag was first placed here on George Washington's birthday in 1907.

service at Mount Rubidoux, where a different country was honored each year.

When you visit, be sure to read the plaque. Added by the Riverside Humane Society in 1934, it honors the personal sacrifice made by Japanese Olympian Lt. Col. Shunzo Kido in 1932. With his horse near death from the 22.5-mile equestrian endurance race, Kido stopped, saving the life of his horse but losing the gold medal. Kido's action remains a fitting symbol of what's required of those who cherish peace and life over victory at any cost.

72

COLTON'S FIRST MARSHALL

What's the connection between Colton and the OK Corral?

The true home of the Earp family is in the 500 block of West "H" Street. Driving that neighborhood provides a sense of what the community looked like at its start, when the Earp family established roots here in 1883. However, you will want to see the full historical record on permanent display at the simply named Colton Area Museum.

The museum houses several artifacts related to other famous citizens and events, but the Earp family connection is one that continues to attract a new audience each generation. For those attracted to cemeteries and tombstones, Morgan Earp's grave marker can be found at nearby Hermosa Cemetery.

Many members of the Earp family came to the area, and other spots, in search of freedom and security. In many ways, their movement across the country mirrors the experiences of many settlers to the area. Seeking more and more opportunity naturally meant moving west. And this part of the state, with large tracts of land surveyed and available for homestead, was a beacon to all walks of life.

The Earp family was similar in this desire to seek out adventure and fortune in the West. A point of pride for the residents of Colton is this significant connection to American folklore. Patriarch Nicholas Earp settled here briefly following the Civil War. In the years after the Battle at the OK Corral in

Relatives of the Earp family still live in this region.

Other connections to this gunslinger past, the Gem Saloon owned by the Earps, the old jail, and "Movieland Frontier Town", have been lost to development and progress in the last few decades. Photo courtesy of Larry Burns.

COLTON AREA MUSEUM

WHAT Artifacts and reenactments of Earp family history, set inside a Carnegie Library turned museum

WHERE 380 N La Cadena Ave., Colton

COST $5 suggested donation

PRO TIP The museum's hours are limited: Wednesday and Friday, 1–4 p.m.; Saturday, 11 a.m.–2 p.m.

Tombstone, AZ, several family members found new starts here.

When Colton incorporated, Nicholas served as a city clerk, and Virgil became the first marshal. He established widely adopted protocols and standards to "tame" what was still, in the late 1800s, a fairly wide-open expanse attracting thousands of new residents annually. Like the Earp family, all of these new residents were eager to make their marks in the mines, in the fields, in saloons, by building infrastructure, or by making something that would encourage others to pack up their lives so they could be a part of it.

73

THE "GRAND LADY" OF THE TEMECULA VALLEY

Welcome! How long will you be staying with us?

Temecula wisely chose to use the historical buildings of the late nineteenth and early twentieth centuries to celebrate its heritage and draw crowds of visitors throughout the year. Old Town Front Street provides blocks of walkable nostalgia. One of its oldest buildings sits right along Main Street, near the gate of this early Temecula Valley settlement.

Care to travel just like they did during this period? If so, the oldest continuously operational hotel in the IE is your place to stay. The Temecula Valley, which served as a crossroads between the more developed areas of Los Angeles County and San Diego County, served the people who grew the food, laid the tracks, and built the structures that attracted thousands of settlers to California. This hotel was front and center for most of that history. As such, it alternately served as the community

HOTEL TEMECULA

WHAT The longest continually operational hotel in the Inland Empire

WHERE 42100 Main St., Temecula

COST $275 and up for a room (weekends only)

PRO TIP Explore the archival collection of historic photographs, newspapers, and related documents during your stay.

Special objects are plentiful here, including the original telephone switchboard for the Temecula Valley.

As the longest continually operational hotel in the region, there's no better way to experience an authentic frontier experience by R.J. and Mary Jane Welty. Photos courtesy of Richard Beck.

Hotel Temecula opened the same year the Southern California Railroad first arrived in the Temecula Valley. It was built on this site in 1883 by R.J. and Mary Jane Welty. Photos courtesy of Richard Beck.

watering hole, restaurant, Red Cross first-aid station, police station, post office, emigration stop, and city hall. This historic structure is yet another example of a place evolving over time to meet the changing needs of a dynamic and vibrant community.

This is a one-stop house of secrets. In its long and storied history, the hotel has had only three owners. The current owners completed a full renovation and restoration of the rooms and grounds in 2014, and the unique layout of the hotel gives you ten custom rooms to choose from. Each one features special artifacts and hidden histories to make your stay memorable—or to make your stay something worth driving for. The garden room features a wisteria patio. The wisteria was the only thing to survive a fire that destroyed the hotel in 1891, a mere two years after it first opened for business.

74

FIRST PEOPLE OF THE IE

Can the desert sustain? If you know where to look and how to cook, yes!

It's a huge point of pride for the Inland Empire that the first museum in California founded by Native Americans is the Malki Museum. Established in 1964 to preserve and promote the earliest human record of this region, the museum continues to grow in prominence and importance. Its programs and exhibitions primarily hold artifacts from the Cahuilla, Kumeyaay, and Serrano, but dozens of tribes are represented here. Some of those tribes were forcibly moved here following the Treaty of Temecula in 1852 or after earlier battles with Spanish and US militaries. Meaning, each piece on display survived repeated annihilation attempts.

Many of those artifacts made it into Jane Penn's care. She found an eager partner to establish this first-of-its-kind museum in Dr. Katherine Siva Saubel. This is another wonderful, home-grown piece of history, safeguarded from extinction by larger forces. On display is nothing less than the tenacious nature of the first peoples of the Americas, secured largely by the efforts of two women.

This museum demonstrates that the tragedies brought in by the Melkish (the Cahuilla word for white man) are bookended by a diverse and powerful history that started in the previous millennium and continues today. That history is catalogued and shared through the Malki Museum Press, another way to amplify their voice and support regional scholarship. The press ensures that Native Americans will have the ability

Food grown in the garden serves as a metaphor for the contemporary Southern California tribes.

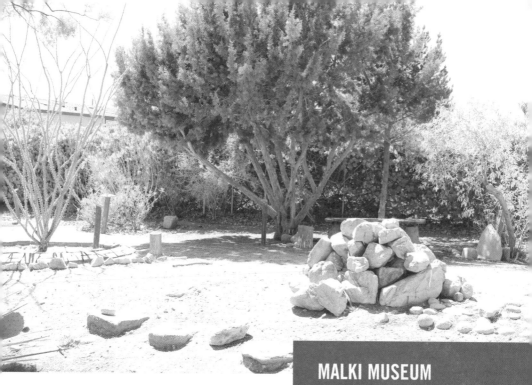

Each exhibit aims to open dialogue and inform visitors of the history, culture and lives of California native Americans in the past, present and future. Photo courtesy of Larry Burns.

MALKI MUSEUM

WHAT Artifacts and garden representing regional cultural history

WHERE 11795 Malki Rd., Morongo Reservation, Banning

COST Free

PRO TIP The Temalpakh Ethnobotanical Garden has all you need to clean a wound, feed a family, fix a roof, or diaper a baby.

to shape their narrative going forward on their own terms, in their own words, and on their own timeline. As such, the museum can be a place to look into the past and the future simultaneously.

Depending on when you visit, you can taste that history and hold it in your hands. For example, the Temalpakh Ethnobotanical Garden demonstrates how to thrive in the desert. With some care, a person can survive on the foods it naturally provides. Annual events like the Agave Harvest and Roast in spring and the Fall Gathering are the best times to immerse yourself in all the tastes.

75 THE TECHNOLOGY MAY CHANGE, BUT THE DESIRE TO HELP OTHERS DOESN'T

Is it accurate to say we "practice" medicine?

Modern medicine evolves so quickly, it may be hard to recall just how much the practices have changed the world. What was deadly in the past can now be treated with a short doctor's visit. Many look to the past as a time of better values and better opportunities. That idea faces serious challenge, however, when it comes to medicine. For example, some wonderful artifacts housed in this medical museum demonstrate how much courage it took just to undergo a medical exam or procedure before the invention of pain medication and sterilization.

Among the displays you'll see here is a surprisingly beautiful group of "bleeding bowls." They're made of various materials, and most bear elaborately painted images or etchings. These and the like are in the "quackery" room, where

Surgical artifacts on exhibition from the Egyptian, Greek, and Roman eras speak a storied history of the healing arts.

The Southern California Medical Museum (SCMM) houses a treasure trove of fascinating medical, dental and pharmacy artifacts, wartime surgery kits, an impressive medical library, medical artwork and photographs, rare and antique bottles that were used to hold and dispense salves, pills, powders and elixirs, unusual and often hard to believe quackery devices and numerous special exhibits. A wide variety of historical periods, geographic locations and medical specialties are represented in the collection. SCMM is the only museum in southern California dedicated to the collection and preservation of medical artifacts and history of medicine. Photos courtesy of Larry Burns.

you can spend hours exploring stories of those "too-good-to-be-true" remedies and "miracle cures" that seem to be as popular today as they were in the nineteenth and twentieth centuries.

On the lighter side, enjoy the exhibit on contraceptive methods. It's hard to say which side was more creative—those aiding pregnancy or those preventing.

More than just a shock to your sensibilities, the museum demonstrates how much progress humanity has achieved in the field of medicine. Appropriately, it's housed on the campus of Western University of Health Sciences' Nursing Science Center. Over the years, it has moved around the Inland Empire—from Colton, to Riverside, and now in the western reaches of the IE, Pomona. The museum has never been easier to visit or better curated, so visit soon.

76 ONE MAN'S CLOISTER WALK IS ANOTHER MAN'S CATACOMB

Is this an underground lair for Mission Revival architecture?

The catacombs beneath The Mission Inn Hotel & Spa had become the stuff of legend even before they were completed. Contrary to popular myth, they did not ferry rum between Mount Rubidoux and the hotel during Prohibition. The earliest references to the hotel's "cloister walks," the proper term for this architectural feature, appear in a *Daily Press* article from 1910 remarking on the hotel's "monastic and catacomb" features. It was popular at the time to build these underground areas and call them catacombs.

Fully developed, the catacombs delivered steamed heat (and a shortcut) to the nearby places of interest and influence for Frank Miller, first keeper of the inn. Miller's mother-in-law was a member of First Church of Christ, Scientist. Hence, that church was the first nonhotel building connected by the catacombs. Next came the First Congregational Church. Then several government buildings— city hall, Loring Building, Federal Building, courthouse, and jail—were added to the system.

In its heyday, each corner of the walk—and this place was chock full of nooks and crannies—told California history through the brushstrokes of thirty-six original paintings by Henry Chapman Ford. These masterpieces were actually saved from the

The original keeper of the inn, Frank Miller, held the patent on the famous Raincross displayed throughout the Inland Empire.

In it's prime, the catacombs housed world class sculptures and paintings. Evening strolls below kept people cool even in warm summer weather. Photo courtesy of Larry Burns.

MISSION INN MUSEUM

WHAT A secret path right under your nose—and feet

WHERE The Mission Inn & Spa, 3649 Mission Inn Ave.; Mission Inn Museum, 3696 Mission Inn Ave., Riverside

COST $13 for a 75-minute museum tour

PRO TIP Free shortened tours available the first Thursday (Riverside Artswalk) and first Sunday of every month.

trash dump—twice! "First friend" of the Mission Inn, Mrs. Patsy O'Toole, fought a days-long battle with a determined housekeeper, Mrs. Peterson, to save the artwork during one of the hotel's dormant periods. The second time she pulled them from the bins, she hid them in an office, where they stayed for decades. A full restoration saved thirty-two of those original thirty-six pieces in the 1990s. They are displayed around the hotel and the Spanish Gallery. You can recognize them by the dilapidated state of their original oak frames. Today, there are few ways to safely view the catacombs, and there's really no reason to do so. Better to glimpse a version of the cloister walk found near the inn's Grand Parisian Ballroom. The closest you can get to that original purpose is the gleaming walkway on your left as you hit the bottom of the stairs. When you visit, hear the full story, and many others, on a docent-led tour at the Mission Inn Museum.

CALIFORNIA'S TRIBUTE TO ABRAHAM LINCOLN

Care to guess which IE museum is OPEN every President's Day?

English immigrant Robert Watchorn arrived in America fifteen years after the death of Abraham Lincoln. But Lincoln quickly became an inspiration to make his dreams a reality. Having worked as a child laborer in the mines, he worked as an adult to improve labor conditions, especially concerning children. Later, he joined many others in the burgeoning oil and gas industries, amassing a large enough fortune to live "part time" in Redlands.

The business success of Robert and his wife, Alma Jessica Simpson, was mixed with personal tragedy. Their first son died in infancy. Their second son, Lt. Emory Watchorn, died after returning home from World War I. For the Watchorns, this death and the death of Lincoln were connected; both gave their lives in service to their country.

LINCOLN MEMORIAL SHRINE

WHAT Only memorial to our sixteenth president west of the Mississippi

WHERE 125 W Vine St., Redlands

COST Free

PRO TIP Tuesday–Sunday, 1–5 p.m. Get a ticket to attend the Watchorn Lincoln Dinner. Held annually in February, it's a full day of scholarly talks on the political, military, and personal life of our storied president.

Forums on the Civil War are held here the second Wednesday of each month by the Inland Empire Civil War Round Table.

LET VS HAVE FAITH THAT RIGHT MAKES MIGHT AND
IN THAT FAITH LET VS TO THE END DARE TO DO
OVR DVTY AS WE VNDERSTAND IT.

ADDRESS AT COOPER INSTITVTE

The animatronic Abraham Lincoln in their display was created locally by Garner Holt Productions, Inc. The patio areas feature excerpts from Lincoln's speeches inscribed into the walls and fountains designed by noted American sculptor Merrill Gage. Photos courtesy of Larry Burns.

Watchorn chose Redlands for his tribute to Lincoln because it afforded an "accessible yet secluded" location. In 1932, the central octagon was raised. Fifty-six years later, the dream was complete with the addition of two new wings, curated exhibits, and expanded archives.

From the Indiana limestone—inscribed plates that line the exterior to the documents and physical artifacts of the Civil War, it is no exaggeration to say there's no other memorial of this scope west of the Mississippi. Additional documents related to this building can be viewed next door in the Heritage Room of A.K. Smiley Public Library.

Another one-of-a-kind feature: a Norman Rockwell original painting, fittingly titled *The Long Shadow of Lincoln*, is among the items on permanent display—without a doubt, the single most valuable artifact in the museum.

78 A FRENCH CHATEAU FIT FOR THE EMPIRE

What garden wonders await your arrival?

The Inland Empire has no royal families, but it does have a princess castle. The 1905 purchase of this property by the Kimberly family tells a familiar Empire tale. After many years "wintering" in the Inland Empire from their native Wisconsin, they wisely chose to make this place their permanent home.

Home building is one of the largest industries of the Inland Empire, and the Kimberly family supported that fact by embarking on decades of development, construction, and, most important, conservation, which we enjoy today. The family's youngest, Mary Kimberly-Shirk, affectionately called "Auntie Bob" by many, grew comfortably into her role as community benefactor. Beyond protecting the estate for future generations, she shaped young minds as president of nearby Scripps College in the early 1940s.

KIMBERLY CREST HOUSE & GARDENS

WHAT Homestead celebrating the "People of Redlands" that captures citrus heritage and long valley views

WHERE 1325 Prospect Dr., Redlands

COST $10 for adults; $5 for children (VIP tours at additional cost)

PRO TIP : Hours: Thursday, Friday, and Sunday, 1–4 p.m. Before or after hours, a short walk up the hill to Prospect Park gives you a commanding view of the Inland Valley. Try it at sunset!

A second estate using the same blueprint was built in Hollywood, now home of the famous *Magic Castle*.

The original grounds included a small orange grove to the north and a fountain, "Venus Rising from the Sea". Dating from 1897, the property is composed of the Chateauesque style residence and carriage house, a formal Italian garden and approximately three acres of citrus. Photos courtesy of Larry Burns.

The chateau and six acres of French-inspired grounds were left to the "People of Redlands," so consider this a stop at an extended family member's house! Stop by in July or August, and get a break from the traditionally warm weather in this cool oasis of live theater, shade trees, and fragrant blooms.

Speaking of flowers, the gardens contain spectacular examples of the plant species that were the must-have discoveries of hobbyists and collectors in the early twentieth century. A must-view is the Grandmother's Sweetheart Garden, named for the heart-shaped Japanese boxwood trees filled with roses. Those roses bloom the sweetest in the spring, but a rose here any time of the year would smell as sweet.

79

A BIT OF KITSCH ALONG ROUTE 66

How many teepee-shaped motel rooms have you stayed in this year?

Its opening in 1949 tells you a lot about this place. One of the great drivers of new residents to this part of California was the end of World War II. The region's patriotic support is evident, from the logistics and communications center in Norco at NAVSEA (Naval Sea Systems Command), to the training facilities north of Barstow at Fort Irwin, and the Marine Corps Air Ground Combat Center at Twentynine Palms. Tens of thousands of men from across the country returned to California bases at the end of their service, and many of them hit the open road.

This site, in addition to providing an unusual rest from the road (there's a classic kidney-shaped pool), offers a peek into the fascinating history of car travel in the American Southwest. As automobiles and roads created new-found freedoms to explore, "autocamping" was wildly popular. As the pastime matured, so did the tastes of the traveler. To accommodate, low-cost motels and hotels sprang up along these new routes, designed not to house immigrants as in the past, but rather a growing class of people called *travelers* or *vacationers*.

The rise of interstates and major commerce corridors made many places along traditional routes like Route 66 into ghost towns. There are spots along the route in the Inland Empire

WIGWAM MOTEL

WHAT Inspired living for those who desire a bit of overnight whimsy

WHERE 2728 E Foothill Blvd., San Bernardino

COST $80–$130 per night

PRO TIP This place is a great base of operations for exploring restored spots along historic Route 66.

Frank Redford built 9 of these wigwam "villages" to house his collection of Indian artifacts. This was the final one built and one of three still standing. Point in fact, these wigwams are actually shaped like teepees, but don't let that detract from a unique travel experience. Photos courtesy of Larry Burns.

that went from boom to bust in the latter part of the twentieth century. This place, the last of its kind in California, survived by being unique, adapting to the environment, and connecting with the community. That recipe is no different than how the earliest Indian settlements—and later waves of immigrants from Mexico, Asia, and Europe—came to call this part of Inland Southern California "home."

This motel is the inspiration behind the "Cozy Cone Motel" in Disney's animated feature *Cars*.

80

DRESSES OF A LOST-BUT-NOT-FORGOTTEN ERA

Is there really a dress for every occasion?

After a visit here, you can watch the next royal wedding with an expert's eye. Those elaborate hats, mysterious veils, never-ending trains, and pieces of flair possess a purpose and significance. Each piece provides a bit of biography on the person who wore it or connects back to the history of the period in which it was created. But even better, you can hear the history straight from the founders, Eve and Steve Faulkner. Eve, a recognized expert on the dress, wedding practices, and social customs of this era, has delivered seminars and lectures worldwide.

Surprisingly, you'll find another era of decidedly US history highlighted: the Civil War. American Victorianism was a cultural period influenced by the values and practices of Northern and Southern aristocracy. It was most prominently displayed

HOUSE OF VICTORIAN VISIONS BRIDAL MUSEUM

WHAT Diverse collection of antique bridal gowns and other artifacts revealing the courtship and marriage practices of the Victorian era

WHERE 146 N Harvard St., Hemet (the Old Hemet Opera House)

COST Free; donations welcomed

PRO TIP The museum is "hidden" inside a storefront that also features a boutique and a dance studio.

If you fall in love with an item, you'll be happy to know that this shop creates stunning reproductions, right down to every stitch and button.

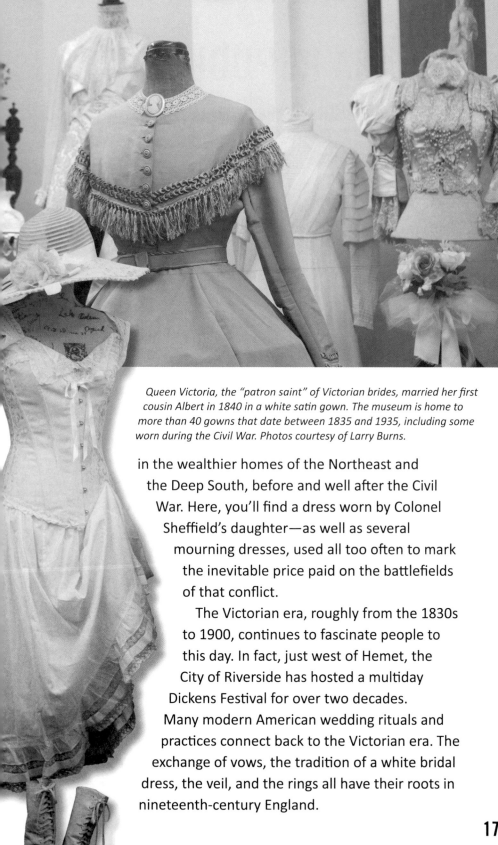

Queen Victoria, the "patron saint" of Victorian brides, married her first cousin Albert in 1840 in a white satin gown. The museum is home to more than 40 gowns that date between 1835 and 1935, including some worn during the Civil War. Photos courtesy of Larry Burns.

in the wealthier homes of the Northeast and the Deep South, before and well after the Civil War. Here, you'll find a dress worn by Colonel Sheffield's daughter—as well as several mourning dresses, used all too often to mark the inevitable price paid on the battlefields of that conflict.

The Victorian era, roughly from the 1830s to 1900, continues to fascinate people to this day. In fact, just west of Hemet, the City of Riverside has hosted a multiday Dickens Festival for over two decades. Many modern American wedding rituals and practices connect back to the Victorian era. The exchange of vows, the tradition of a white bridal dress, the veil, and the rings all have their roots in nineteenth-century England.

81

BANANA REPUBLIC

Can you say "banana" without smiling?

With a little detective work, most of the odd sites found around the Inland Empire eventually make sense. A remote and dilapidated motel in the middle of nowhere might have been the place to be until a new highway diverted traffic elsewhere. The mystery woman who places a large metal sculpture in the middle of a desert landscape might be trying to convey a message about the space between things.

INTERNATIONAL BANANA MUSEUM

WHAT A museum that showcases all things banana

WHERE 98775 State Hwy. 111, Mecca

COST Free

PRO TIP Do you feel heavier here? At 235 feet below sea level, it's the second-lowest point in California.

But a banana museum—and an international one no less! Lots of food is grown here, but nobody's planting bananas. That didn't stop the International Banana Museum, however, from relocating to the shores of the Salton Sea at Mecca in 2010. The connection here is family. The museum's proprietors, Fred Garbutt and his wife, Kym, have ties to the Salton Sea dating back over half a century.

The museum earned a Guinness World Record in 1999 in the category of world's largest collection dedicated to a single fruit. The award is well deserved, because the museum artfully maximizes every inch of real estate to showcase most of the twenty thousand items shaped like, made from, or inspired by the naturally happy fruit.

Your visit will make you smile—especially if you're a banana lover. But be sure to call ahead (619-840-1429) for maximum happiness. Hours vary by season, but the museum is typically open on weekends and some other days when the sun is shining.

Be sure to sample the foods while you are here—a seemingly endless variety of breads and shakes will engage all your senses during your visit. With over 20,000 banana related items, it's the worlds largest collection of items dedicated to a single fruit. Note, the banana is NOT native to Southern California! Photos courtesy of Fred Garbutt.

The nearby Salton Sea is the largest lake in California. *Audubon California* considers it "one of the most important places for birds in the Western United States." It's worth a visit.

82

HINDU TEMPLE, SWAMINARAYAN BRANCH

Why is a stunning example of Indian architecture alongside Highway 71?

The Inland Empire has a connection to hundreds of ethnic groups, religious traditions, and ways of living. It's the secret behind the IE's success – new ideas, new people, new energy! This site captures what's interesting about the present and the future of Inland Southern California.

Bochasanwasi Akshar Purushottam Sanstha (BAPS) is a Swaminarayan branch of Hinduism. The branch has a significant presence in the United States, and this center is one of five North American temples. Although it isn't the largest— that nod goes to Jersey City's temple—it could be argued that it's the most ornate and welcoming of them all.

The temple is an interesting mixture of keeping tradition and connecting with the modern local community. Two proofs of that. First, there's a monitored security gate at the entrance, but the person stationed there couldn't be nicer or more welcoming. Then, there are the solar panels that generate electricity, located to the left of the entrance. These panels provide all the power for this place—and more. What this temple doesn't use is put back into the grid for the benefit of the entire community.

Most people breeze through the lobby to get to the temple. But take time to observe the craftsmanship required to create

---

This temple is described as the "floating" Mandir because the seismic technology below ground will keep it "afloat" during the next big earthquake.

The lower floor of the Mandir is home to an interactive exhibition on the history, culture and wisdom of Hinduism. Visitors can learn about the origin, beliefs, and values of Hinduism, and how this ancient religion is thriving today throughout the world. Photo courtesy of Larry Burns.

BAPS SHRI SWAMINARAYAN MANDIR AND CULTURAL CENTER

WHAT Temple, educational facility, and cultural center

WHERE 15100 Fairfield Ranch Rd., Chino Hills

COST Free

PRO TIP Take a self-guided tour during regular visiting hours: Daily, 9 a.m.–noon and 4–7:30 p.m.; or a private Saturday tour, offered 10 a.m.–noon and 4–6 p.m.

the soaring lobby walls, as well as the exterior walls, completely covered in ornate, hand-carved teakwood replete with symbols of elephants (representing strength and vegetarianism) and the peacock (bravery and patience). The marble of the temple itself—from the Nagpur region of India—is similarly hand carved.

During visiting hours, you may see active private-worship services. But even with people doing walking meditations along the outer walls, or folks sitting cross-legged or laying prostate before one of a half dozen altars honoring the four gurus of BAPS, the temple is surprising easy to navigate.

83 THE HIDDEN BENEFITS OF DRINKING FOUNTAINS

What does it take to keep men out of saloons?

Ontario's temperance fountain is a secret hiding in plain sight. It was moved to its current location in 1975. Built in 1908, it was originally situated about three miles north, and likely outside a saloon. These days, thousands of commuters pass it daily without knowing what it is.

TEMPERANCE FOUNTAIN

WHAT For some, it's still cool to "Just say no."

WHERE "C" St. and Euclid Ave., on the median, near the bandstand, Ontario

COST Free

PRO TIP The Ontario fountain still works, but the sprayer is temperamental. It could shoot in any direction.

One reason is its placement along the grass median of a divided highway. A second reason is its design. The large, rough stone construction bears little resemblance to a modern day drinking fountain.

Two national issues explain why temperance fountains began to "spring up" in the early 1900s. The first was the women's suffrage movement, which would result in the nineteenth amendment to the Constitution, giving women the right to vote. The other issue was the temperance movement, which sought to remove alcohol from society, thus creating a freer and kinder community.

What's a temperance fountain? It provided an alternative to the saloon. Hard to believe, but in the 1900s, clean drinking

Temperance fountains were a visible representation of a stronger female voice in America's political life in the early 1900s.

Besides keeping men out of saloons, fountains serve as reminders that some of the greatest resources can be shared for free. With no set design, temperance fountains can be found across the country, and no two are alike. Most were locally commissioned and produced. Photos courtesy of Larry Burns.

water was hard to find. So a well-intentioned man might enter a bar for a glass of water, only to be tempted by the devil's elixir. The fountains were a way to prevent those weak menfolk from succumbing to peer pressure by keeping them out of the bars altogether.

There's a second temperance fountain, a replica, in Chino, at the corner of Sixth Street and "D" Street. That one was created by the Women's Christian Temperance Union (WCTU) in the 1890s. The WCTU is still an active club, with 103 members as of 2013.

84 CHILDHOOD TOYS ON PERMANENT DISPLAY —HOORAY!

Which single toy best represents your childhood?

The curator and creator of this place, Jim Griffin, has a passion for the little big trucks that are iconic images of many American childhoods. The fascination with big machines often starts when we are young. As this display of 920 Tonka toys demonstrates, the appeal can last a lifetime.

Many of these toys were "rescued" from the trash heap or the dusty corners of many a garage. The impressive collection is spread across two adjoining lots.

Visitors may wonder why the collection is displayed outdoors. The answer is simple: there's no place out of the elements to house all the toys currently in the collection. And the outside placement lets people come by anytime they like to take a photo at the fence. Besides, as Griffin notes, they're indestructible. Sure they may rust outside, but they won't drift into obscurity.

Visitors are limited to the fence line, but Griffin loves to talk about his passion for collecting while you're clicking away on

---

TONKA TRUCK GRAVEYARD

WHAT Over 900 Tonka trucks at the ready

WHERE 5069 Bain St., Mira Loma (just south of Fiftieth Street)

COST Free

PRO TIP Look for the "Tonka Trucks Only; All Others Will Be Bulldozed" sign when you park.

Other Tonka related toys are in the collection, but the trucks are center stage and the only items visible to the public from the street. Photo courtesy of Larry Burns.

your cell phone. This active, involved guy is known to have given away a Tonka or two for worthy children's causes. His interest in little trucks comes naturally: he spent a lifetime driving trucks and was a four-time national champion in his field. He also found time in the 1980s and 1990s to run for elected office, first for US president and later for the Senate.

A closer look uncovers the evolution of this American icon over the decades.

OTHER FUN YOU CAN FIND IN A GOLF CART

How has the sport of golf influenced culture?

If the automobile made modern America, then you could say the golf cart has irrevocably shaped the look and feel of this part of the Inland Empire. People from out of state find this part of the IE especially attractive because the pleasant winters here provide year-round outdoor recreation. One of the most popular is golf.

There are two swaths of green common in most of our desert communities. The first you'll find are the crops. Most of the winter food grown in the United States comes from California. The southeastern part of the state—with its flat topography, consistent climate, large workforce, and access to fresh water is an ideal spot for agriculture.

The second cause for the desert greening is the sport of golf. This part of the Coachella Valley boasts one of the larger concentrations of golf courses in the country. In light of all the golf, it was only a matter of

PALM DESERT GOLF CART PARADE

WHAT An annual October celebration of community history, arts, recreation, and imagination

WHERE 72559 State Hwy. 111, Palm Desert

COST Free to watch; nominal fee to enter a golf cart float

PRO TIP Check the parade route maps to determine the spot you want to be to watch. And be sure to bring plenty of sun protection; it can still run into the nineties here well into October.

In lieu of flowers, these floats are decorated with colored tissues.

Think of a mini Rose Parade where the carts are decorated with tissue paper instead of roses. Then add bands, clowns, and other marching groups; a cultural celebration like no other! What started as "Christmas in July" for the benefit of local residents who found the summers boring, today it attracts tens of thousands every Fall. Photos courtesy of Palm Desert Area Chamber of Commerce.

time before some folks realized those little carts could be loads of fun on actual city streets.

What started between a few locals in the 1960s slowly grew into a regional tradition. Just about any group can apply to join the parade. The only catch is that your participation in the parade must include a golf cart decorated to the theme for that particular year.

86 FAIRY TALE-INSPIRED ARCHITECTURE

How might the world look if it was settled by gnomes?

Turning onto this street, a person is immediately struck by a feeling that something is different here. Those of a certain age may feel they've walked onto the set of their own private *Twilight Zone*. What you're likely noticing is the scale of this street. Each of these eighteen Normandy-style cottages was the creation of a former Hollywood set designer.

Having retired from the film industry, this craftsman and artist created an avenue to rival the sets included in a tour of Universal Studios Hollywood. The street feels narrow, the houses closer together. It's fascinating to see how the nearby dream factory of Hollywood influences even the architecture of this early IE community.

Taken together, the place does seem ideal for those of below-average build. But perhaps this sense of the small comes from the fact that the people and places of the Inland Empire may have grown over the last century. We're bigger, so our stuff is bigger. These homes, perhaps, speak not to a secret gnome enclave or retirement community of the *Wizard of Oz* Munchkins, but rather to a past where the world was metaphorically smaller.

What each homeowner has done is amazing. Some embrace the concept wholeheartedly. For example, there are homes with several other smaller "gnome homes" or "fairy cottages" hidden about the property.

When visiting, be mindful that this is a residential neighborhood near a public school. Please park outside the block in designated areas and stay on public rights of way.

In a 2018 episode of "Restored", host Brett Waterman preserves one of these treasures, and makes a quick side trip to get supplies from "Weber House" in Riverside. Photo courtesy of Larry Burns.

Would you believe people were retiring from the film business in 1926?

GNOME HOMES

WHAT Homes made with a touch of Hollywood magic

WHERE Near McKinley Elementary School, at the corner of West Clark Street and Normandie Court, Redlands

COST Free

PRO TIP This is a residential street. Please be respectful of residents. Do not enter private property or remove any items.

87 CELEBRATE THE SEASON OF GIVING

Spreading Christmas cheer along historical trade routes

In 1958, the community of Ontario noticed a lack of holiday spirit and decided to take action. As all great solutions start, they called on an artist—in this case, Rudolph Vargas. The East Los Angeles artist created a series of crèches, models or tableaux representing the life of Jesus Christ, based on his previous work for the city of San Diego.

From a small first-year unveiling for local boosters, the event became a regional tradition, with thousands visiting each year to walk or drive Euclid Avenue. Quickly growing, more crèches were added, eventually bringing the total to twelve.

CHRISTMAS ON EUCLID AVENUE

WHAT Dozens of holiday displays and vendors along Euclid's wide, grassy median

WHERE Corner of "B" Street and Euclid Avenue, Ontario

COST Free

PRO TIP You'll encounter smaller crowds midweek. Displays and vendors are in place for viewing in mid-November and remain through New Year's Day.

On arriving to take in the displays, pause and marvel at this rare highway's layout. It puts people first. The location was ideal because of the large grass median dividing this north-south route—it covers more real estate than the actual road. Take it all the way north, and you end up in Mount Baldy, the easiest peak to spot in the San Gabriel Mountain range. Hint: It's the one sporting a chrome dome.

Today, the twelve scenes are just one part of the dozens of displays erected by private citizens

Christmas on Euclid started in 1922, and the Nativity Scenes were added in 1958. Photo courtesy of Greater Ontario Convention & Visitors Bureau.

and nonprofit groups to celebrate the diversity of our community and the season. There are tableaux representing many faiths and belief systems. Everyone is welcome. Bundle up and walk parts of Euclid to view the craftsmanship up close. Additionally, you can plan your visit around the various "reindeer games" taking place across the holiday season. Tree-lighting ceremonies, parades, singalongs, and snowballs are a mere sleigh ride away.

This annual multicultural event celebrates all the reasons for the season in the IE.

88

A FITTING CAR FOR A FINAL JOURNEY

Does how we travel say something about who we are?

Trains once represented the safest, most convenient, and most cost-effective means of travel across the wide expanses of California. This region grew up on agriculture and tourism, and the rails made those industries possible. Starting in the 1950s, however, the railway's dominance faced serious decline. Its competition? Revolutionary interstate highways, providing several smooth lanes to speed folks across the landscape in personal, individualized comfort.

That decline resulted in the mothballing of several rail lines and related equipment. Groups interested in the preservation of this era's transportation artifacts, former railroad workers and engineers, slowly collected land and cars and historical documents. Today, the Orange Empire Railway Museum attracts thousands of tourists to ride the trains for education and entertainment.

The funeral car housed here represents the value and necessity of the train as it relates to urban development. As cities became crowded, burial practices changed in the United States. More cemeteries appeared not in city centers or near churches, but on the outskirts of towns. Funeral train cars became the preferred

WORLD'S LAST FUNERAL CAR AT THE ORANGE EMPIRE RAILWAY MUSEUM

WHAT Where modernity meets death

WHERE 2201 S "A" St., Perris

COST Free to tour the grounds and museum; $8 and up for weekend (only) train rides, 11 a.m.–5 p.m.

PRO TIP The annual "Day Out with Thomas" draws thousands of little fans each November. Hours: Monday–Friday, 9:30 a.m.–4:30 p.m.; weekends, 9 a.m.–5 p.m.

In 1912 the all-day 150-mile Orange Empire Trolley Trip from LA included stops in San Bernardino, Riverside (with lunch at the famed Mission Inn) and Redlands before return to LA in the early evening. The Descanso (originally known as the Paraiso) was part of the Los Angeles Railway, or Yellow Line, which at its peak comprised twenty streetcar lines with 1,250 trolleys. Photos courtesy of Larry Burns.

way to deliver mourners and the casket to the dearly departed's final resting place. These elaborate cars provided a smooth, "conditioned-air" ride, much preferred to the often bumpy and unreliable roads of the early twentieth century.

This particular car, The Descanso, provided decades of service, earning its own final resting spot. After funeral car lines were replaced by modern roads and the ubiquitous hearse of today, this car was reincarnated as a place for travelers to rest as they came through the Cajon Pass. But modern cars that didn't require a rest after braving "the pass" put The Descanso out to pasture for good. The pasture in this case is a nice warehouse, where this one-time funeral car sits in all its reconditioned elegance.

When you visit, quiz your conductor! They love sharing what they know about these trains and their place in California history.

In 1920, $3.50 would buy a round-trip train ticket from "the east" to the "Orange Empire."

89

A PLACE WHERE THE JOURNEY IS THE DESTINATION

Does it feel like we've been waiting for the mail to arrive all day?

MOJAVE ROAD MAILBOX

WHAT A pointless—but fun—mailbox on an important road

WHERE Mojave Road, Mile Marker 74, Mojave National Preserve

COST Free

PRO TIP For some history on the area, as well as modern amenities like food and water, head to the Kelso Depot Visitors Center about an hour away at 90942 Kelso Cima Rd., Kelso.

This mailbox exemplifies a recurring experience in the northern Mojave. A wild idea is hatched, resources are secured, then interesting characters are lured into the mix. Add in a bit of luck, tenacity, and experience—and, ta da, a cultural experience is born!

The person credited with spearheading this "mail drop" is Dennis Casebier, who stayed following the completion of his military service at Marine Corps Air Combat Center in Twentynine Palms. Owing to the dozens of military installations across the Inland Empire, from the earliest Spanish outposts to present day, many of the people who call this place home do so because their military service required it.

The Mojave Road was a crucial route for those traversing this part of the Inland Empire. It was one of the earliest trade routes, established by Native Americans and expanded under Spanish explorers. Thinking of this road as tributary, it was one of the sources that brought to the IE the people, ideas, and material goods required to build and shape this community.

The name [Mojave] is composed of two Indian words, aha, water, and macave, along or beside. Aha denotes either singular or plural number. Mojaves translate the idiom "along or beside the water," or freely as "people who live along the water (river)." The mailbox is a wonderful way to be noticed and keep to yourself while you explore the natural beauty of the Mojave desert. Photos courtesy of John Marnell, Mojave Desert Archives, Goffs, CA.

Given the rich history and significance of the road, efforts started in the 1970s to support it as a recreation destination, not unlike the Pacific Crest Trail. Realizing the 130-mile road would be unsuitable for hiking, the driving surface was improved over several years by volunteers, leading to the creation of the Friends of Mojave Road, as well as a few books on the subject. As a bit of fun, and a way to keep tabs on traffic and use, the group of volunteers established a "mailbox," never an official postal designation.

Visit and sign the book, read other messages, or send a note. Your note will never reach its destination, of course, but you came out to the desert to get lost, not found—right?

The Friends of Mojave Road erected this bit of joyful absurdity.

90

THE BATHTUB RING OF THE COACHELLA VALLEY

Where did all the water go?

The history of the Inland Empire can be explored through thousands of artifacts left by previous cultures and immigration waves. But sometimes the juiciest secrets are left out in the open for us to discover, if we only know where to look. To see this particular secret, you need to get to Highway 86, at the western and southern "edge" of the Inland Empire.

Other entries in this book reach back several, or even a hundred, years. A few interesting secrets had their origins thousands of years ago. Heck, the oldest living object in the Inland Empire is a tree that's at least thirteen thousand years old. So strap in tight, because we're jumping back in time a million years (or more!) for this secret.

"Ancient Lake Cahuilla" broadly refers to the various freshwater lakes that have appeared and evaporated literally thousands of times since the Pleistocene age. In more recent times, three hundred to five hundred years ago, parts of it were referred to as "Lake Leconte" on old maps.

The original footprint roughly covered the delta along Mexico's northern border to Indio, over two thousand square miles. Those old lakes left behind a mineral called travertine. A freshwater lime deposit found at historical lake shorelines,

Some believe the name "Coachella" was a misspelling of the Spanish word for a crustacean's shell, "conchilla." Found abundantly in area mountains and desert floors, they are additional evidence of this ancient gargantuan lake.

Fishing traps found miles from the current lake edge speak to the recent history of this massive lake. Photo courtesy of Larry Burns.

WHAT Evidence of an enormous freshwater lake

WHERE Travertine Point at Hwy. 86, Desert Shores

COST Free

PRO TIP At the corner of Hwy. 86 and Coolidge Springs Rd., look west toward the mountains, then east to where the lakeshore currently sits.

travertine is light-colored and easy to spot against the darker pigments of the Santa Rosa Mountains to the north and west of the Salton Sea.

In addition to the plentiful geographic evidence, there are fragments of fish traps along some of the water marks, used by Cahuilla Indians as far back as four hundred years ago.

There's evidence—which is to say, more travertine—along the mountains north of Indio and to the west of La Quinta. But this spot, at the southern edge of Riverside County, provides a clear view for a look-back into the IE.

SOURCES

Citations listed in order by appearance in the book.

One [Baseline] to Rule Them All
https://www.highlandnews.net/entertainment/baseline-base-line-or-baseline-
road/article_58224ace-928d-51e9-942b-9d0d83246c2e.html
Interview with Doug McCollough on 6/5/18

The Badland's Jack Rabbit Trail
https://www.pe.com/2014/02/27/
back-in-the-day-jackrabbit-trail-was-a-first-link-between-moreno-and-redlands/

Milta Café: Alpha y Omega
http://www.mitlacafesb.com/
https://la.eater.com/2015/1/30/7952807/
san-bernardino-mitla-cafe-history-taco-bell-feature-photos
Interview with Irene Montano 10/6/18

The World's First McDonald's Restaurant
Research Links and notes: Various interviews with Phil Yeh and Albert Okura.

Home of the Flaming Hot Cheeto
https://youtu.be/WadWS1JJeEo
http://www.ssdachurch.org/about

Shields Date Garden
https://youtu.be/HSHPQWyxZds

The Secret Sauce of the Fast Food Industry
https://www.kcet.org/socal-focus/fast-food-industry-has-inland-roadside-roots
https://www.sbsun.com/2013/04/16/
wienerschnitzel-story-had-its-roots-in-inland-empire/

Candy Candy Everywhere
http://www.loganscandies.com/candydemos.php
Visit and interview with Jerry Rowley on 9/26/18

The Relevancy and History Project at California Citrus State Historic Park
Based on original research by Megan Suster and Frank Taylor, as part of the
Relevancy and History Project, a partnership between the University of California,
Riverside, and California State Parks. The pilot project at California Citrus State
Historic Park focuses on migration and immigration and highlights hidden
histories of people and place. It includes new research, partnerships, student
participation, community story collection, outreach events, and exhibitions.

The Mormon Rocks at Cajon Pass
https://patch.com/california/redlands/mormon-period-built-region-in-early-years
https://www.fs.usda.gov/Internet/FSE_DOCUMENTS/stelprdb5391972.pdf42
https://www.fs.usda.gov/recarea/sbnf/null/recarea/?recid=26543&actid=62

The Fire Lookout at Tahquitz Peak
https://www.fs.usda.gov/recarea/sbnf/recarea/?recid=71977
Interview on 6/17/18 with Bob Romano and Charles Phelan, US Forest Service
volunteers

Hemet Maze Stone
http://articles.latimes.com/1991-06-11/news/mn-515_1_hemet-maze
https://www.californiahistoricallandmarks.com/landmarks/chl-557
http://www.ancientpages.com/2016/06/24/baffling-prehistoric-maze-stones-in-hemet-
    and-san-jacinta-valley-california/

Chaney Hill
https://www.facebook.com/MurrietaLifestyles/videos/988447334643965/
Interview with Jeffrey Harmon on 9/15/18

The Arrowhead
http://ohp.parks.ca.gov/ListedResources/Detail/977
http://www.sbcity.org/about/history/arrowhead_springs_hotels.asp

Heart Rock Trail
https://www.hikespeak.com/trails/heart-rock-hike-san-bernardino-mountains/
http://www.cityofcrestline.com/heartrock/

San Jacinto's Ephemeral Mystic Lake
http://www.northfriends.org/images/feb.14.newsletter/Feb.2014newsletter.pdf

Mentone Beach
https://www.redlandsdailyfacts.com/2011/01/04/
    mentone-has-roots-as-a-resort-colony/

Cross Country Skiing
https://rimnordic.com/trail-system-info

Children's Room, Corona Public Library
Interview with librarian Abby Schellberg on 9/6/18.

The Abandoned Pedley Powerhouse
Interview with Kevin Bash on 9/10/18 and Bash, Kevin and Angelique Bash. A brief
    history of Norco. The History Press. Charleston, SC, 2013.

Samuelson's Rocks
http://cali49.com/jtnp/2013/10/22/samuelsons-rocks

Barstow Murals
http://www.mainstreetmurals.com/map.htm

The Edward Dean Museum and Gardens
https://www.edward-deanmuseum.org/
Interview by phone with Bradley Harjehausen on 8/23/18

Cabot's Pueblo Museum & Toth's Wooden Indian Head
http://www.cape-coral-daily-breeze.com/page/content.detail/id/504893.
    html?nav=5036&showlayout=0
http://www.cabotsmuseum.org/about-us/

East Jesus
http://eastjesus.org/

Natural Boulders as Sliced Apples
https://travelinspiredliving.com/
    rock-art-roadside-attractions-apple-boulders-of-perris-california/

Water Park Gone Graffiti Art Enclave
http://www.moderndayruins.com/2008/01/rock-hoola-water-park.html

Noah Purifoy's Outdoor Desert Art Museum
Noah Purifoy site brochure "Noah Purifoy Outdoor Desert Art Museum of Assemblage Sculpture"

Elmer's Bottle Tree Ranch
https://bottletreeman.blogspot.com/
Interview with Elmer on 8/4/18

The Inlandia Poetry Library
Interview with Nikia Chaney and Ernie Garcia on 7/6/18

The Maloof Home
Interview with Connie Ransom, docent 9/28/18 and Jim Rawitsch, executive director at Maloof Foundation on 10/5/18

Cove Artist's Colony at Cathedral City
http://coachellavalleyweekly.com/
cathedral-city-cove-walking-tour-artists-historic-homes/
Interview with Peter Palladino, president of the Agnes Pelton Historical Society on 10/27/18

Peanuts Spike Statue
https://schulzmuseum.org/timeline/
http://www.mohavedailynews.com/news/coming-home-needles-chamber-gets-ok-for-spike-statue/article_4eb0f3f0-1e04-11e4-9959-001a4bcf887a.html

Sunvale Village, A Community for the Small
Interview and tour with Cathy Allen on 6/6/18

The Tale of Ramona and Alessandro
https://www.sandiegoreader.com/news/1988/sep/29/cover-was-ramona-real/?page=1&
http://ramonabowl.com/

Weber House
http://oldriverside.org/weber-house/

White Lines
http://articles.latimes.com/2006/apr/24/local/me-a2anniversary24

UCR's Herbarium Answers Your Question—Is This Dangerous?
http://herbarium.ucr.edu/Herbarium.html
http://oltw.blogspot.com/2011/02/13000-year-old-oak-of-inland-empire.html?m=1
http://journals.plos.org/plosone/article?id=10.1371/journal.pone.0008346

Goldstone Deep Space Complex
https://www.gdscc.nasa.gov/

DonkeyLand
Interview with Amber LaVonne, founder of DonkeyLand on 9/11/18
Interview with John Welsh, Riverside County Animal Services communications manager on 10/17/18

Serrano Tanning Vats
Dana Jr., Richard Henry. Two Years Before the Mast. New American Library, New York. 2009.

Old Woman Meteorite at Desert Discovery Center
Interview with Jane Laraman Brockhurst on 10/25/18
"Old Woman Meteorite" brochure from US Department of the Interior BLM

Mill Creek Hydroelectric Plant
https://www.hydroworld.com/content/dam/hydroworld/site-images/
2106_HallofFame.pdf

Cal-Earth
http://www.calearth.org/

Garner Holt Productions, Inc
Interview with Garner Holt on 7/13/18

Desert Studies Center
http://nsm.fullerton.edu/dsc/
http://nsm.fullerton.edu/dsc/desert-studies-about
http://calstate.fullerton.edu/titan/2003/zzyzx/

John Rains House
http://www.sbcounty.gov/museum/branches/rains.htm

The Integratron
https://www.integratron.com/

Secret Training Camp for Pearl Harbor Retaliation
Interview with Harry Geier, director of marketing and development at Planes of Fame,
10/26/18
https://www.sbsun.com/2017/09/18/
inland-empire-fliers-part-of-attack-on-japan-after-pearl-harbor/amp/
http://www.planesoffame.org/

The San Bernardino Cannon
https://www.ci.san-bernardino.ca.us/about/history/jumuba.asp
https://www.pe.com/2010/07/24/open-wide-and-say-bang/

The George S. Patton Memorial Museum
www.generalpattonmuseum.com
https://www.deserttrainingcenter.com/
Interview with James Soliz, staff at museum on 9/14/18

Battle Line of the Mexican American War
https://www.hmdb.org/marker.asp?marker=379

BibleLand's Stone House @ Temecula Creek Inn
http://www.temeculahistoricalsociety.org/html2/bibleland.html
http://www.sandiegouniontribune.com/news/columnists/logan-jenkins/sd-no-jen-
kins20170612-story.html
https://temeculacreekinn.com/wp-content/uploads/2017/02/Stone-House-History.pdf

Pioneertown
John Huff, A View From Pioneertown
My House With 19 Rooms

Cisco Kid Was A Friend of Mine
"Pioneertown" brochure, date unknown.

Ruddy's 1930's General Store Museum
Interview with Sally McManus on 10/27/18

First Jail Cell in Southern California
http://www.ci.san-bernardino.ca.us/about/history/first_jail.asp
Interview with Lyn Killian on 9/19/18

1925 Elsinore Firetruck Engine #1
Interview with Ruth Atkins, director of Lake Elsinore Historical Society on 5/16/18

Gilman Ranch and Wagon Museum
http://www.rivcoparks.org/gilman-historic-ranch-and-wagon-museum/
Trans-Polar Fight Puts San Jacinto on the World Stage
https://www.stamp-collecting-world.com/USSR_F1.html

Walk the Spanish Trails
Interview with Nancy Melendez, executive director of Old Spanish Trails (CA), on 2/6/18.
http://www.sbcounty.gov/museum/branches/agua.htm

Cucamonga Service Station
https://route66ieca.wildapricot.org/servicestation
Interview with Luana Hernandez, volunteer on 9/29/18

Motte Historical Museum
Interview with Maria Mathey-Marckstadt, general manager on 8/4/18
http://www.mottemuseum.com/

Amboy, Living Ghost Town
Interview with Albert Okura, aka "The Chicken Man," on 7/11/18

Museum of Pinball
http://www.museumofpinball.org/about-us/

The Norconian
Interview with Kevin Bash on 9/18/18
http://www.lakenorconianclub.org/history/
https://youtu.be/MY6zwkLFdSk

Santa's Village at Skypark
https://skyparksantasvillage.com/
interview with Brad Lofland, public relations and marketing manager, on 10/21/18

Vinyl Film Festival
Interview with David Young on 10/31/18

Spadra Cemetery
Interview with Deborah Clifford, President of Historical Society of Pomona Valley on
    9/13/18

Healing Buddhas of Adelanto
http://www.thienvienchannguyen.net/
Interview with Thich Dang "Tom" Phap (on-site monk) and interpreter Phuong Pham on
    7/1/18

(Lake) Elsinore Grand Prix
Interview with Steve Miller, event director, on 10/10/18

The Peace Tower and Friendship Bridge
http://www.totallymtrubidoux.org/history/
http://evergreen-cemetery.info/people/frank-augustus-miller/

Meet Virgil Earp, Colton's First Marshall
https://coltonareamuseum.com/

Hotel Temecula
Interview with Richard Beck, owner, on 10/14/18

Malki Museum
Interview with Amanda Castro on 8/16/18
http://malkimuseum.org/

Southern California Medical Museum
Interview with Susan Purdy, docent, on 9/13/18
http://www.socalmedicalmuseum.org/About-The-Museum

Catacombs of the Historic Mission Inn and Spa
Interview with docent Barbara Burns on 1/26/18
Mission inn newsletter https://mail.google.com/mail/u/0/#label/IE+Secret/1611ede0ad
    cbcb9f?projector=1&messagePartId=0.1

California's Tribute to Abraham Lincoln
http://www.lincolnshrine.org/the-watchorns/

A French Chateau fit for the Empire
http://kimberlycrest.org/

The Wigwam Motel
http://wigwammotel.com
Interview with Samir Patel on 9/5/18

House of Victorian Visions Bridal Museum
http://www.victorianbridalmuseum.com/

The International Banana Museum
http://www.internationalbananamuseum.com/about-the-museum-1.html
Interview with Fred Garbutt, owner, on 9/29/18

BAPS Shri Swaminarayan Mandir and Cultural Center
https://www.baps.org/Global-Network/North-America/LosAngeles/Mandir-Info.aspx

Temperance Fountain
https://www.historicalmarkerproject.com/markers/HMP36_wctu-fountain_
    Ontario-CA.html

Tonka Truck Graveyard
https://youtu.be/cMGmDmIW8ww

Palm Desert Golf Cart Parade
http://golfcartparade.com/about-the-parade/history/

The Gnome Homes
Interview with Lucas Cuny, film studies professor at San Bernardino Valley College, on
    7/2/18

Christmas on Euclid Avenue
https://christmasoneuclid.com/about-us/

World's Last Funeral Car at the Orange Empire Railway Museum
https://www.citylab.com/transportation/2013/05/
    funeral-car-named-descanso-or-when-death-rode-rails-america/5478/
http://www.oerm.org/history-of-the-museum/

Mojave Road Mailbox
http://www.mdhca.org/about-mdhca/our-history

Lake Cahuilla Bathtub Ring
Interview with Phil Rosentrater, director of Salton Sea authority, on 7/9/18
http://www.sci.sdsu.edu/salton/AncientLakeCahuilla.html
https://www.redlandsdailyfacts.com/2011/01/04 mentone-has-roots-as-a-resort-colony/

INDEX